WHITEHEAD AND HIS PHILOSOPHY

A.H. Johnson

UNIVERSITY
PRESS OF
AMERICA

LANHAM • NEW YORK • LONDON

Copyright © 1983 by

University Press of America,™ Inc.

4720 Boston Way
Lanham, MD 20706

3 Henrietta Street
London WC2E 8LU England

ISBN (Perfect): 0-8191-3460-0
ISBN   (Cloth): 0-8191-3459-7

TO MY GRANDFATHERS

WHITEHEAD AND HIS PHILOSOPHY

Acknowledgements

I acknowledge with gratitude, permission granted by The Macmillan Publishing Co. New York, to quote from the following books by Alfred North Whitehead: Science and the Modern World (Copyright, 1925, by The Macmillan Co.); Religion in the Making (Copyright, 1926, by The Macmillan Co.); Process and Reality (Copyright, 1929, by The Macmillan Co.); The Aims of Education (Copyright, 1929, by The Macmillan Co.); Adventures of Ideas (Copyright, 1933, by The Macmillan Co.); Modes of Thought (Copyright, 1938, by The Macmillan Co.).

I am also grateful for permission to quote, to Cambridge University Press, co-holders of copyright on the following A.N. Whitehead books: Science and the Modern World, Religion in the Making, Process and Reality, Adventures of Ideas, Modes of Thought.

Included in this book are some materials which have already appeared in professional journals. I appreciate the courtesy of the editors who have allowed me to quote, as requested, from: (a) Allison H. Johnson, "A Critique of D. Bidney's 'Spinoza and Whitehead'". The Philosophical Review, XLVII, No.4, 4 July, 1938, reprinted by permission of The Philosophical Review; (b) A.H. Johnson, "The Psychology of Alfred North Whitehead", The Journal of General Psychology, 32, (1945); (c) A.H. Johnson, "Whitehead as Teacher and Philosopher", Philosophy and Phenomenological Research, Vol. 29, No. 3, 1969.

Charles Hartshorne has allowed me to reproduce the contents of several letters which he wrote to me over a period of approximately 40 years. I have reproduced six letters from Alfred North Whitehead to me. Years ago the late Professor T. North Whitehead, on behalf of his mother (A.N. Whitehead's literary executrix) sanctioned and supported my use of available Whitehead material, "at his disposal". My gratitude to Charles Hartshorne and to the Whitehead family is profound.

Brief quotations from other sources are appropriately acknowledged in footnotes.

The publication of this book has been made possible by a grant from the J.B. Smallman Fund of The University of Western Ontario. I am most grateful to Assistant Provost Dr. Andrew K. Bjerring and the members of his committee for their prompt and favorable response to my request for assistance.

My manuscript emerged into legibility thanks to the efforts of several members of the secretarial staff of the Department of Philosophy, University of Western Ontario. I am particularly indebted, in this regard, to the skill and goodwill of Mrs. Pauline Campbell, who prepared the "camera-ready" final copy. My wife, Helen, has rendered much appreciated invaluable assistance as proof-reader and literary adviser.

This book is dedicated to my Grandfathers William Howard Heartz and David William Johnson. I grew up in the home of one and also had close association with the other. The passing years have brought deepening appreciation and gratitude.

A.H. Johnson
The University of Western Ontario
London, Canada.

WHITEHEAD AND HIS PHILOSOPHY

TABLE OF CONTENTS

INTRODUCTION

A

This book is based on the results of over 50 years
of "concern" with the philosophy of Alfred North Whitehead. It embodies the "fruits" of extensive discussion
with Charles Hartshorne at Chicago, and Alfred North
Whitehead at Harvard, in the mid 1930's. It has had
the benefit of the rich treasury of Whitehead scholarship through the years. In this regard the work of
Charles Hartshorne and of Victor Lowe merit special
mention. This volume is a supplement to my Whitehead's
Theory of Reality and Whitehead's Philosophy of Civilization.

Whitehead and His Philosophy contains three major
sections: (I) a "word picture" of Whitehead as teacher
--his personality, methods and "what he taught". This
is designed to "set right" some sadly mistaken notions
which are sometimes expressed or implied (Chapters 1-4);
(II) a corrective discussion of some major recurrent
specific difficulties, and errors, involved in the interpretation (understanding) of Whitehead's technical
metaphysical theories (Chapters 5, 6); (III) an attempt
to correct two crucial general errors--namely, (i) the
widespread neglect of the fact that the basis of Whitehead's philosophy is a series of insights (intuitions)
which he expresses (a) sometimes in highly technical
terms (words) and concepts, but also (b) alternately, in
more ordinary fashion; (ii) extensive neglect of the vast
scope of Whitehead's philosophy (Chapters 7-9).

B

The relevance of this three-fold project is obvious
when one examines the present state of Whitehead studies.
(I) There are a number of conflicting "reports" concerning the personality of Alfred North Whitehead, and
in particular his "performance" as a teacher of philosophy. These reports range all the way from a claim of
"near perfection" to the designation: "miserable inep-
titude". A careful examination is needed in order to
settle this issue.

(II)   A major difficulty in understanding <u>Process</u>
<u>and Reality</u>, and some parts of its companion volumes:
<u>Science and the Modern World</u>, and <u>Adventures of Ideas</u>,
arises from the fact that his technical terms and
concepts are unfamiliar even to most professional
philosophers.   However, this difficulty can be overcome, or at least lessened, if it is realized that
there are two relatively clear and "easy to understand"
thought models used by Whitehead: (a) a moment of human
experience, (b) a pulse of electrical energy.

    Whitehead himself admits that sometimes he has
trouble in expressing his insights.   Hence his statements are inadequate--vague and lacking in detail.
Some of his comments on "objectification" are a case
in point.   There are other sources of difficulty in
understanding Whitehead's philosophy.   He sometimes
uses a single term in several different senses, e.g.
"eternal object", "feeling".   Also he is not always
careful in stating what he means by a technical doctrine
--or in using technical terms.   Examples are: his remarks on creativity and the functions of God's primordial and consequent natures.   Indeed, Whitehead sometimes makes a sweeping unqualified general statement--
then later imposes extensive restrictions and qualifications.   In any case, he is quite prepared to admit
that some of his technical concepts and theories require
revision.

    It is very important to bear in mind these dif-
ficulties, and note Whitehead's own warning that one
should try to get a comprehensive understanding of
what he is saying.   In other words, one should avoid
an uncritical concentration on an isolated statement;
note that relevant theories gradually develop as to
detail.   Only thus will a person acquire a sound basis
on which to try to understand Whitehead's ideas on
various topics.

    Arising out of these difficulties there are a
number of recurrent errors concerning Whitehead's
philosophy.   A representative sample will now be
mentioned in order to indicate, further, the topics
which will be discussed in this volume.

    One of the most serious misunderstandings of
Whitehead's theory of God's primordial nature is the
claim that God imposes its subjective aim on a newly

arising actual entity--at least in its initial form.
Also, a number of interrelated errors arise concerning
Whitehead's theory of the consequent nature of God. It
is wrongly claimed that in God's consequent nature all
(otherwise) past actual entities are everlastingly
retained--in their entirety--without loss.

A strange neglect of the fact that Whitehead's
thought underwent a considerable process of development, leads to fruitless discussion. It is set in the
context of outmoded earlier analysis. It is apparently
not realized that this analysis is later replaced by
another one, though strangely the latter material is
brought to bear, but in distorted form--because of its
use in outmoded context. Specifically, in Religion in
the Making it is stated that there are three "formative
elements" in the universe: creativity, ideal elements
(subsequently termed "eternal objects") and God. A
dispute has arisen as to which, if any, of these has
priority. This, incidentally, has been taken by many
to imply (or to state) that creativity is a basic,
indeed the basic, and most fundamental factor in the
universe. All this, obviously, does not take seriously
Whitehead's later, more mature, position that actual
entities are the final real things of which the universe
is made--that God is one actual entity among others--
that all actual entities manifest creativity, i.e., it
is a characteristic of actual entities, hence not an
independent concrete substantial entity which is the
source of actual entities, or the material out of
which they are made. Eternal objects (including the
eternal object: creativity) constitute one of the main
ingredients of the universe.

Whitehead's lack of care in stating his real point
of view--and hence the misunderstanding (error) on the
part of some of his "admirers", is illustrated by his
remark that everything is process (reality is process).
That Whitehead provides a very fundamental and extensive qualification of such statements--is frequently
overlooked--or at least not taken very seriously.

As in the case of many technical presentations,
some persons purporting to discuss Whitehead's theories,
content themselves with a "mere repetition" (in the form
of extensive quotation or slight changes of a few words
of Whitehead's own statements). This frequently implies, or illustrates, a lack of genuine understanding
on the part of the "repeaters". For example, it is not

realized by many, that when Whitehead is talking about "the two-way functioning of eternal objects", thus providing a link between actual entities--it is not eternal objects as pure potentials, but eternal objects which are exemplified, that he is discussing. Also when it is reported that according to Whitehead an actual entity positively prehends all other entities-- the required qualifications are omitted: Contemporary and future actual entities are not positively prehended. Further, and paradoxically, so-called positive pre- hension has as an ingredient negative prehensions. Chapters 1 and 2 of section I are relevant to these matters as discussed in the preceding paragraphs.

(III)   Some serious errors occur concerning Whitehead's categoreal scheme as outlined at the be- ginning of Process and Reality (pp. 27-42). The cate- gories (concepts) are falsely assumed to have an ultimate status, such that mention is made of what the categories require Whitehead's philosophy to be. This extreme rationalistic interpretation simply flies in the face of Whitehead's contention that categories are descriptive--expressions of basic insights (intuitions).

In section III, in view of errors involved con- cerning Whitehead's general approach to categories, and the lack of realization of the scope of his philo- sophy--three chapters are included. One (Chapter 7) attempts to (a) focus attention on the importance of intuition (immediate experience) in Whitehead's philo- sophy, (b) consider examples of intuition, (c) consider the basic categories (concepts) which are reported to be justified by intuition. (d) A concerted attempt is made to emphasize the fact that there are two sets of categories in Whitehead's philosophy, one technical, the other "ordinary". Chapter 8 is devoted to showing, by way of some examples, how Whitehead makes use of his non-technical categories in a wide variety of ways. In other words, the applicability of ordinary cate- gories to the many areas of human experience, covered by Whitehead's philosophy, is demonstrated. Chapter 9 offers criticisms of, and suggestions concerning, Whitehead's theory of God,--in the context of a continuing discussion of the two categoreal schemes.

This volume concludes with an Epilogue entitled: "Through Fifty Years". It is a sketch of the author's associations direct (i.e. as a Harvard student) and indirect (i.e. through his writings) with Whitehead.

It provides background which may be of assistance in understanding, and evaluating, the interpretations of Whitehead and his philosophy found in this "study".

This book contains some criticisms of defects in the philosophy of Alfred North Whitehead. Already mentioned were: (a) his use of one term in several different senses, (b) carelessness in stating the exact meaning of, or using, some of his basic concepts or theories. In addition (c) attention is called to some internal inconsistencies--for example in his discussion of God as an actual entity. Further, it is suggested (d) that his technical categoreal scheme is defective on two counts: (i) it does not cover some data, (ii) it does not apply appropriately to some data to which Whitehead refers it. Also (e) he neglects some relevant data. (f) Whitehead is sometimes vague or lacking in details in crucial statements.

However, the central purpose of this book is not to engage in negative criticism of the philosophy of Whitehead. Its excellences far exceed its defects. This book is mainly concerned to correct a number of recurrent crucial errors, in attempts to understand (interpret) Whitehead and his philosophy--on the part of a number of "Whitehead Scholars" and other members of the philosophical community.

C

It may appear that I take issue chiefly with interpretations of Whitehead presented by my revered teacher Charles Hartshorne and by Professor W.A. Christian. However, by disagreeing with them, on specific technical, and on general, points, I find myself in opposition to a very large number of men and women who approach Whitehead along trails blazed by one or the other of these distinguished scholars. The reasons for differing from Hartshorne and Christian are stated, as clearly as I can, in passages in, or referred to in, this volume.

My corrective discussions, of errors in under-standing Whitehead, made by Hartshorne and Christian, apply equally to those who emulate these influential philosophers. For the purposes of this book, I have not considered it necessary to list names and articles, and/or books, of such persons. The crucial point here is to identify and correct some major errors. Names

and work of the outstanding chief exponents of errors
under consideration are introduced in order to bring
the errors into clearer focus.

In the case of a number of widespread errors
which are not perpetrated by Hartshorne and Christian,
no outstanding originator, or chief exponent, is
involved. Hence, usually, no names or sources are
introduced. However, in the case of several distinctive (not widespread) errors, names of individuals
are mentioned, for example Pols and Feibleman. In
the project of portraying "Whitehead as Teacher", Paul
Weiss and others who present varying views on this
topic are mentioned, to indicate the nature of the
problem.

In brief, this book does not propose to provide
a complete, detailed, "rogues gallery" of whose who
perpetrate errors in understanding Whitehead's philosophy. It is not an exhaustive catalogue of men and
their work in this field. It is, to repeat, an attempt
to identify and correct a number of major errors concerning Whitehead and his philosophy. Thus the fact
that I have not mentioned a number of persons, nor
referred specifically to their work--should not be
interpreted as indicating a neglect of any phase of
Whitehead scholarship.

Specifically, it may be objected that by paying
considerable attention to Hartshorne and Christian,
there is excessive concentration on one part of
Whitehead scholarship, and not enough interest in
contemporary developments. It is true that the important work of Hartshorne and Christian, to which I
refer, was published a number of years ago--yet its
influence has continued to the present day. Indeed,
some of Hartshorne's basic ideas on Whitehead have
been reiterated by him recently. (See Process Studies,
Vol. 10, numbers 3-4, 1980, pp. 93-94). The ideas of
Hartshorne and Christian on Whitehead as expressed by
others at the present time are, in a real sense, contemporary. Similarly, the information concerning
Whitehead and his philosophy in my article, "Whitehead
as Teacher and Philosopher" published in 1969 (Philosophy and Phenomenological Research, Vol. 29, No.3),
and reprinted as part of Chapter 2 of this volume, is
still contemporary in the sense that it is still
relevant to issues presently under discussion. It
will be noted that some of the issues discussed in
this volume involve material published very recently.

I have included, as part of Chapter 2 of this volume, my 1969 paper on "Whitehead as Teacher" because it is a detailed report of some of my experiences as a graduate student at Harvard in 1936-37. Specifically, I was writing a Ph.D. thesis on "Whitehead's Theory of Actual Entities", under his supervision. This report provides an accurate "picture" of some aspects of Whitehead's philosophy and the methods he used as teacher and supervisor of a Ph.D. thesis. Because of its context and content, this chapter serves as a reliable presentation of many of the basic ideas of Whitehead's philosophy. Crucial questions were asked. Whitehead gives clear and direct responses. Finally, the "previously published" material of Chapter 2 is reproduced here because it seems appropriate, indeed advisable, to make it readily available, in view of references made to it in this volume.

Incidentally this chapter is rich in so-called "one-liners", i.e., penetrating aphorisms which drive home important points by "well turned" phrases. Many of these one-liners are characterized by ironic humor. (Note is taken in the Index of similar aphorisms in other chapters of this book.)

It is, of course, the case that some of my criticisms of errors in the understanding (interpretation) of Whitehead's philosophy have the support of some other philosophers. The same is true of some of my criticisms of the philosophy of Whitehead as such. However, I have not, in this book, identified this support. That is so because here my concern is to demonstrate the nature of these two sorts of errors (defects) and correct them when possible. This requires, ultimately and crucially, a careful examination of Whitehead's actual "performance", i.e. what he said and wrote.

In this book attention is focused on Whitehead and his philosophy. No attempt is made to deal with distinctively, exclusively theological issues. However, of course, some philosophical discussions have theological implications.

In quoting from Whitehead's writings, first editions have been used. I have derived benefit from the "Corrected Edition" of Process and Reality (D.R. Griffin and D.W. Sherburne, editors, The Free Press, New York, 1978).

However parallel pagination, referring to both editions would have made the text of my book unduly cumbersome. In any case, the vast majority of the changes in the "Corrected Edition" do not have a crucial bearing on the phases of Whitehead's philosophy here under discussion. When relevant, the "corrections" have been taken into consideration.

Abbreviation Symbols

In most instances, when references are made in this book to pages in volumes by Alfred North Whitehead--standard abbreviation symbols will be used, as follows:

S.M.W. Science and the Modern World, The Macmillan
        Co. New York, 1925.

R.M.   Religion in the Making, The Macmillan Co. New
        York, 1926.

Symb.   Symbolism: Its Meaning and Effect, The Macmillan
        Co. New York, 1927.

P.R.   Process and Reality, The Macmillan Co. New York,
        1929.

A.E.   The Aims of Education, The Macmillan Co. New
        York, 1929.

F.R.   The Function of Reason, Princeton University
        Press, Princeton, 1929.

A.I.   Adventures of Ideas, The Macmillan Co. New York,
        1933.

M.T.   Modes of Thought, The Macmillan Co. New York,
        1938.

Two edited collections of essays by Whitehead are symbolized thus:

"I.S." Alfred North Whitehead, The Interpretation of
        Science (edited by A.H. Johnson), Bobbs-Merrill,
        Indianapolis, 1961.

"W.A.E.S.P." Whitehead's American Essays in Social
        Philosophy (edited by A.H. Johnson), Harper,
        New York, 1959; Greenwood Press, Westport,
        Conn., 1975.

It is convenient to provide symbols for three other books to which reference is made in several chapters in this volume:

W.T.R. A.H. Johnson, Whitehead's Theory of Reality,
        Beacon Press, Boston, 1952; Dover Publications,
        New York, 1962.

W.P.C. A.H. Johnson, Whitehead's Philosophy of Civi-
        lization, Beacon Press, Boston, 1958; Dover
        Publications, New York, 1962.

E.R.   A.H. Johnson, Experiential Realism, Allen & Unwin,
        London; Humanities Press, New York, 1973.

Symbols used only within a single chapter will be iden-tified at the end of the chapter in question.

SECTION I

WHITEHEAD AS TEACHER

CHAPTER 1

WHITEHEAD AS LECTURER

I

During his career at Harvard, Alfred North Whitehead chiefly supervised and instructed graduate students in philosophy. He also dealt with undergraduates. In 1936-37, in addition to the individualized tutorial responsibilities described in the following chapter, he lectured to a "mixed bag" of undergraduates and graduates (chiefly the former) on "Cosmologies" (Fall 1936) and "The Function of Reason" (Spring 1937).

The "Professor Whitehead" who appeared in the large lecture theatre at the rear of the first floor of Emmerson Hall, was a man "stooped with age", a bit less than average height. He spoke slowly in a voice which revealed his English ancestry. His eyes were a sparkling blue, his cheeks rosy. An almost bald head retained a fringe of white hair about the level of his ears. He appeared as a venerable, friendly grandfather type of person. Some, impressed chiefly by his "hair-do", suggested that he looked like a saint whose halo had slipped!

At this time Whitehead's physical energy was somewhat diminished. He arrived by taxi at Harvard Square, entered the Yard by the Johnston Gate and then walked across to Emmerson Hall--a distance of a few hundred yards. His return to his apartment in Radnor Hall, on the Charles River, was the reverse of his arrival process. Frequently Whitehead sat at a desk on the lecture platform. However, he was perfectly capable of pacing about on the platform in a very energetic fashion. In any case, there was no lack of obvious intellectual vigor and enthusiastic commitment to his assignment as teacher.

He usually began his lectures with a crisp statement of his theme or topic. At the end there was a summary or humorous anecdote. All through his lectures there were brilliant turns of phrase and flashes of humor. He was particularly impressive in providing simple illustrations bearing on the topic under discussion--sometimes very technical ones.

1

There were those who found it difficult to "follow" the Professor.--He "jumped about" from one subject to another--sometimes without any apparent relational link. However, the more perceptive members of his audience usually could "see" that he was appropriately implying (using) relationships which are ordinarily overlooked.

Whitehead preferred to use the class hour for lecturing. Few questions were asked or invited during this period. On the other hand, at the end of the class hour he was very willing to remain a while and discuss issues raised by members of the class. He fielded questions with skillful good humor. His efficiency in general human associations, and his ability to stimulate and instruct in a one to one relation, were demonstrated when he entertained students in his home. Unfortunately these social occasions were rare in his later years because of the state of his health.

It seems appropriate to supplement and support the preceding general sketch by providing a "reconstruction-summary" of the highlights of some typical Whitehead lectures on "Cosmologies" and on "The Function of Reason" (based on lecture notes taken at the time). Most of what is presented here are the actual words found in my notes. The order of presentation as well as the content have been carefully preserved. As an aid to understanding, there are background comments, and the introduction of connecting terms in order to provide a more grammatically appropriate literary form.

II

On October 24th, 1936 in the course of discussing Lucretius On the Nature of Things, he remarked that this poem gives evidence of the influence of country life. For example, concerning the origin of things, it is claimed that they originate from the earth, ultimately by a process of mixing. In a sense, this is a doctrine of evolution.

Whitehead quickly noted that the references to God or Gods in this context, are not to be taken seriously as explanatory of the phenomena of nature.

2

ather, references to traditional notions are simply
eremonial, such references are merely ornaments of
iscourse. Lucretius was dedicated to the seculari-
ation of Roman life.

With evident relish, Whitehead told the following
tory: During the First Punic War against the Cartha-
enians, a Roman admiral manoeuvered his enemies into
"bottle-neck" bay and with wind and weather in his
avor, he was prepared to sail in and achieve a great
ictory. But he decided to do the ceremonially
ppropriate thing, and consulted the "sacred chickens"
o see if there was a divine sanction for his proposed
ssault. The priests, in great agitation, reported
hat the sacred chickens would not eat. Therefore it
as impossible to proceed with the battle. The admiral
istened with apparent respect and then said: Let us
ind out whether the chickens will take liquid nourish-
ent. He threw them into the sea; they drank copious
mounts of water. The admiral, satisfied that suffi-
ient respect had been shown for religion--proceeded
o achieve his victory!

Lucretius was convinced that there was emergence
f complex qualities, indeed of life itself, from a
imple background. He offered as proof the observed
act that life emerges from solid, inert matter--for
xample worms appear out of a dung heap.

Whitehead then engaged in what might seem to be
 digression, but he regarded it as a necessary and
seful background comment. He remarked that the
odern point of view concerning nature coordinates
an and the animal world. Emotions are fundamental.
e receive from immediate experience emotional atti-
udes. We do not see something, make an intellectual
djustment, and then generate emotion. More speci-
ically, Whitehead offered the following analysis of
xperience: 1) emotional experience, 2) flashes of
nalysis disclosing objects of such experience,
) concentration of attention on qualities of objects
n abstraction. The earlier point of view would
ssign primacy to item 3). Whitehead suggests that
ur senses have developed to enable us to make ab-
tractions. Sense experience is not a reliable source
f information about fundamental facts--emotion has
hat status.

3

Returning to the evolution theme, Whitehead remarked, concerning the Universal Theory of Emergent Evolution: Bringing rabbits out of a hat is exactly the meaning of Emergent Entities. One must so describe ultimate facts as to make emergent evolution possible. In Whitehead's opinion Lucretius didn't do that.

Specifically, to claim that a "huddle" of atoms produces co-ordination, indeed that any thing is produced by atoms, is a silly superstition--just as absurd as to claim that there is a god in a tree (to account for its functioning)--when no god is seen by anyone.

So Whitehead states that we must seek descriptions which are rational, in the sense that the things described require each other, so that if you understand the environment you understand how things arise. This understanding is beyond us. We do experience flashes of understanding. We must trust to simple identical flashes of understanding.

On November 5th, 1936, Whitehead's topic was "The Mathematical Method in Philosophy". He began by pointing out that in the 17th century there was a vast change in the "common sense" (i.e., generally accepted) attitude toward the world. He remarked that (1) at this time men "started with a kick at the Middle Ages" but didn't realize what they owed to this period in world history; (2) Scholars stressed the importance of mathematicians--said they were following a mathematical method. Though they did not introduce mathematical details, they did use general ideas derived from mathematics; (3) Great discoveries make it important. More specifically, there was a new handling of quantitative (mathematical) notions: Algebra, differential calculus, geometry (a) projective geometry, (b) analytic geometry.

You find all this embodied in Descartes, Spinoza, and Leibniz. In the case of Leibniz, a monad is formed by its formula which is its very being. It really is a particle travelling a curve. Space is a mode of harmonization.

Whitehead then offers an "aside" to the effect that "there is never only one source for a great idea". It may arise from one source, but it is made

4

effective by a second, because it is made interesting by a third--and so on and on.

Incidentally said Whitehead, returning to Leibinz for a moment--Newton's concept of the "sensorium of God"--how God saw things together--is very much like the Leibniz "pre-established harmony".

Continuing his discussion of the importance of mathematical method, Whitehead stated that Euclid, Archimedes, Kant (organization of bases of experience) all had mathematical interests. --"With Kant (i.e., after Kant) mathematics passed out of philosophy (i.e., for a time)." To illustrate this point Whitehead remarked "I did begin to read Hegel, I confess--but I found his mathematical discussion to be utter bosh".

In the 19th century and subsequently, Whitehead reminds us, there was a great revival of interest in the generalities of mathematics, and in logic as a related discipline. He mentioned Boole, Gaussmann, W. Hamilton, De Morgan and pointed out that some of these were "many-sided" men with interests other than mathematical. Benjamin and C.S. Peirce, also Peano were noted, in passing, as well as his Harvard colleagues: Lewis, Sheffer, and Huntington. In whimsical fashion, concerning mathematics and logic, he warns against generalizing "till you haven't got mathematics or logic"! His former student, and colleague, Bertrand Russell was not forgotten. He remarked that "Bertie" was a "tremendous genius--but there were limitations".

With a twinkle in his eye and a chuckle, Whitehead remarked that Hume was reported to have never had a fuzzy idea in his head--but, said Whitehead "there is danger in clarity; I always comfort myself with that thought".

In more serious tone, Whitehead returned to a familiar theme: we must transcend the common sense of an epoch, yet retain rational coherence of ideas. Toward the end of this lecture, by way of summary, Whitehead added some comments on the psychology of periods when the method of mathematics is prominent. Men seek to evoke rational doctrines from the inspection of antecedent phases of experience. This is the Baconian method: look at facts--evoke doctrines.

Concerning Francis Bacon (and his method), Whitehead offered the criticism that this is all very well
and apparently useful but Bacon didn't bother about
facts or discover anything (by this method). In
facetious mood, Whitehead remarked that the only
effect of Baconian observation of facts (on one occasion) was his own death! One day his coach ran
over and killed a venerable hen. He decided to check
the refrigeration powers of snow. So he personally
stuffed the fowl and placed it by his feet in the
coach. The fowl was well preserved. Bacon caught
cold and died! Anyway, said Whitehead quoting the
usual jibe: Bacon wrote of science like a Lord Chancellor, i.e., in a completely autocratic fashion--
of course for a time he was Lord Chancellor of England.

Man seeks to understand, that is develop, a
rationalized system (coordinated system of essences)
and with this, in imagination seeks to use it as an
explanation of subsequently observed data. Yet,
comments Whitehead with exaggerated pessimism, this
is a selective process: arbitrary in nature. There
never has been fully accurate observation.

Whitehead began his November 19, 1936 lecture by
stating a then widely held philosophical view (which
he himself didn't accept): "Let us put aside unfruit-
ful speculation--that is, let us return to Descartes".

Whitehead described Descartes as analyzing the
world into high grade mentality at one end of the
scale, and matter at the other. His attitude to this
view is frequently expressed by his comment: "Good
God, what a gap!" He went on to remark that the gap
is bridged by another fact of experience (Life in all
its stages is as far as you can go in the process of
examination.) Indeed, said Whitehead, the "gap" concept is like looking at a stick--seeing both ends
only--disregarding the stick!

By way of background Whitehead then proceeded to
define several key terms as follows:

Learning: scholarship, clear and distinct observation

Common sense: direct observation, common to humanity

Rationalization: trying to get an enlarged understanding of the interconnections of things (a) limited
(b) unlimited

He then stated what he regarded as a fundamental principle of procedure: Always ask questions beyond convenient stopping places.

In this context he remarked that mathematics has done a great deal of harm. It gives an excellent set of static ideas. We know all about them. Mathematics seems to rise from given foundations.

Genuine knowledge is approximation, not a complete group of data. When so-called knowledge analysis is clear, it is because we have not asked a sufficiently penetrating question.

Mathematics has the merit of asking questions which go beyond immediate experience. "Mathematics has the flavor of being a little mad". "Hasn't mathematics arrived at a stage where we had better stop it"--Aristotle probably thought that. Continuing in this fashion he jokingly remarked: "Metaphysics shows serious defects. There is always a broad minded asking of questions beyond common sense."

Whitehead then turned to consider the meaning of the notion: "together". He recalled that Hume claimed that a thing is nothing but a collection of qualities. However, according to Whitehead, Hume at least occasionally "knew better". He realized that if one adds another quality to the collection it is still the same group because (or if) the principle of unity is the same. Hence a "thing" is not merely a collection of qualities. Unfortunately Hume usually neglected this important fact. Whitehead is prepared to claim that each collection requires its own "principle of union". This goes beyond common sense--which is confined to groups of things.

Whitehead then suggested: In answering questions about "limitation to common sense"--look for examples in the history of Chinese civilization. It stopped lead at a certain point.

He concluded the lecture with a humorous story concerning a reaction to his philosophy. In an early book he used the word "urge" in a "substantive" sense. An archdeacon of the Anglican Church said: "That's the sort of language you'd expect from a 2nd rate female novelist." In this fashion, chuckled Whitehead, metaphysics is "hounded" by unappreciative critics!

In his spring 1937 course on "The Function of
Reason" Whitehead did not restrict himself to various
epistemological themes. He dealt also with background
relevant metaphysical topics. Thus on the 23rd of
March 1937, he began by stating that reality is not
one but many. He proceeded to state that process (on
which he placed considerable emphasis) has two aspects:
1) the stream of history--in general, out of which new
actualities arise. The process of entrance into new
immediacy is important. It is to be noted that "new"
has an exciting quality. One shouldn't represent time
by a line of points--each of which is a "present".
An entity (reality) is the activity of receiving the
stream. 2) The activity of self-formation is another
factor in process. The reality is the continuity of
self-formation (with reference to past and future).

Newton's introduction to the concept of a passive
piece of matter was most disastrous: A consideration
of actions and interactions is not necessary in order
to understand nature. The law of gravitation is a
secondary matter. We are reminded of Newton's famous
phrase "I believe (accept) no hypotheses--only observations". Whitehead went on to remark that he (Newton)
had observed sun, moon and planets--and things like
books and stones, yet he never considered a situation
in which one of the bodies was not a heavenly body or
the earth. He never took two small bits of matter and
proved that they attracted each other--yet he said "I
believe no hypotheses".

In an aside, Whitehead remarked that "overstate-
ment of what he has seen and done may be the defining
characteristic of man".

Returning to comments on Newton, and setting up
a comparison between his theory of reality (theory
of actual entities) and that of Newton, Whitehead
reports that Newton talks about process (reality) but
doesn't say what's going on. On the other hand Whitehead regards an actual entity as the togetherness of
many realities and the unity of one stream. If you
insist on (emphasize) the unity of stream it makes
an actual entity a qualification of a unity beyond
itself.

Whitehead then pointed out that Behaviorism is a natural adjunct to Newton's view of nature.

Having introduced a psychological theory (issue) Whitehead proceeded to refer to Descartes' famous mind-body dualism. Nature is a "stoggy" fact, no activity is required. On the other hand there is mentality which is an essential activity. Thus arises the "appalling problem" of the body and mind.

The solution by Behaviorism is to regard mind as an epiphenomenon: "It is taken away in the rubbish basket."

Whitehead's approach in general is this: In modern science (in contrast to Newtonian science) the gap between activity and inertia doesn't exist. Nature (matter) and mentality are both recognized as actuality. Is there any essential gap? Whitehead replied that he can't find a genuine gap anywhere in nature--no matter how low you go. Stream of activity is basic. The reputed stogginess of matter is a misconstruing of what is persistent in our experience.

Solidarity of nature is the most evident fact of our experience when we are wide awake. But wide awake experience is the most alterable, unreliable part of our experience. Some sense experience does not convey stogginess. Hearing gives you a sense of activity.

On the face of it, the most evident qualities are those which have least noetic worth, namely those qualities which can most easily be got rid of. Sight abstracts from the totality of the world in which we live. "For God's sake shut your eyes and consider how your experiences are arriving from the antecedent state of mind and body." (Don't open your eyes and begin looking at things.)

Whitehead finished his lecture by making some apparently random comments. He suggested that light exercise, food and yachting are better than going to the doctor. Plato liked yachting--everything changes on the sea. Plato couldn't make up his mind to start with stogginess or activity. (Thus he returned to an earlier theme!)

Both Galileo and the Inquisition overstated the truth. In certain cases (i.e., points of view) both

9

are true (i.e. inertia stogginess and activity).
Spatial relations are relative. There is no absolute
space.

Whitehead began his lecture of <u>March 25th 1937</u>
on the Function of Reason, by sketching the outline
of a six point analysis of the development of an
ultimate unit of reality--a so-called "actual entity".
It ran as follows:

1) Derivation from the past
2) Carrying on--conformation
3) Sampling
4) Adjustment--arrive at unity from contributions
5) Sense of prolongation or maintenance
6) Future

Throughout there is "enjoyment". That is: how you
are feeling. Real fact is "subject now". Sense of
influence of enjoyment of the future is enjoyment of
what you will be when immediacy is past.

Whitehead then offered some remarks on philosophy
in general. He stated that philosophy has suffered
horribly from elaborate contributions of high grade
learning derived from the study of foreign languages,
i.e., philosophy has been built on a study of learned
words. In Whitehead's opinion philosophy should not
leave out anything. However, as a matter of fact,
the technical language of the sciences prevents us
from enjoyment of immediacy of experience in other
fields. Philosophy has got away from ordinary
immediate experience. It should be concerned to get
away from abstractions.

Whitehead then initiated a series of reflections
on "History". He made points concerning history:
(1) It is one stream--one historic world, (2) It is
the togetherness of many final absolute realities,
e.g., my own self <u>now</u> activity of feeling.

You (anyone) have had experience of being <u>one</u>
among many things. We experience our individuality.

The problem arises as to how to understand the
stream of the many and the one. In Whitehead's
opinion "inflow" is the explanation of how many
actualities become one history. A new individual

unity (constituting an actual entity) is derived from the inflow of many actualities and enjoyment of the future.

Yet it still seems problematic. How can one actuality in fact enter a new actuality as a datum?

Whitehead begins by reminding us that sense experience is clear and distinct yet it is escapable. Therefore don't put your trust in such experience. As far as we can observe creatures, there are many animals which don't experience sense data. But they do have a sense of feeling derived from (a reaction to) the immediate environment.

Whitehead shrewdly remarks that "expectation is the best instrument (weapon) for exact observation. If you do not have rigorous expectations you will miss almost everything.

He expressed the opinion that we have never been adequate in our philosophical premises, therefore we have to appeal to authority. One of these is habit. It would take 125 years to acquaint oneself with other points of view with reference to a problem. We can't stop and consider all alternatives. (In the midst of all this Whitehead remarked that "The Dialogues of Lucian are the best reading going".) A person's action depends on: habit, training and intuitive judgment.

He then returned to his discussion of the relation of one actual entity to another. Speaking technically, it is a case of "objective" immortality of one in the other. He suggests that (1) there is the past actual entity providing data for the new one, (2) there is feeling by the new subject (i.e., actual entity) of those data. The feeling must involve confrontation, i.e., shared by the two entities.

In answer to the question: Is there a basis in human experience for this technical doctrine of objective immortality? Whitehead replies: Consider a person's experience of his immediate past. If you were bored 1/20 of a second ago, you are still bored. This continuity of feeling gives rise to the notion of "identity".

On April 15th, 1937 Whitehead noted that a
summary of his position on value was available in
an article by G. Morgan in The International Journal
of Ethics, Vol. 49, 1936, pp. 309-16.

He proceeded to point out that the Benedictines
saved Western Christianity from mere individual soul
saving by an emphasis on social activity. Agricul-
ture and learning were both given a practical orien-
tation. This was one of the crises in civilization.

Aesthetic enjoyment which embraces totality in
unity (i.e., in the case of an individual) embodies
the main element in ethical life. "Civilization dies
of boredom--and boredom arises from too narrow
interests."

A sense of social responsibility is basic in all
levels of life. We must make an effort to condition
the environment. In general we must go beyond one-
self--into self-forgetfulness.

In our intellectual activities, in an effort
to achieve the good life, there is always to be
considered a "double notion": (1) there are things
that can be apprehended intellectually; (b) there
are "historic accidents". The division between the
two has been too finely drawn.

Whitehead then turned to a brief discussion
of the problem of class membership. He asked the
question concerning class human; and class animal:
How are their members together? He points out that
members of different classes are together in different
ways, e.g., men and the Ten Commandments. Also there
are different senses in which things form a class
(how together). This is one of the basic (if not
the basic) problems in philosophy.

Whitehead then returned to a theme which occurred
several times in the course of his discussion of the
function of reason: Final truth can only be expressed
by an "infinite intelligence", i.e., based on the
view of the entire universe (i.e., have a connected
Universe)--can't have separate entities.

We can see the "truth-making" presuppositions
as far as the background which we are unable adequately

to analyze. We have vague recognition of the general nature of the backgrounds. That is the secret of induction. When you ask what will happen--any propositions you formulate are based on presuppositions of existence of matter of the sort we have to deal with in our experience.

IV

The immediately preceding "reconstructions" of Whitehead's lectures demonstrate that he was perfectly capable of expressing himself in the lecture hall, in a clear, relatively simple, organized and efficient fashion.

On occasion, however, Whitehead introduced "more technical" material than that referred to above. Also there were moments when even the most favourably inclined had difficulty in finding much continuity in Whitehead's presentations--except that the diverse topics were all of interest to the lecturer; and the apparent disorder was merely an indication of the complexity of a topic.

For example, in his lecture of March 30, 1937, Whitehead plunged into a discussion of "the conceptual functioning of an actual entity". As a first step, he offered some comparative background remarks about physical prehensions. Specifically, he noted that physical prehension is a process of conditioning --to that extent a controlling of the character of the immediacy of the present. On the other hand conceptual prehension is teleological.

He then suggested that a simplification involves a background of interest (or bias). Whitehead stated that he can't understand how people come to think that the universe is simple.

He then moved on to some comments on eternal objects. The "object" ingredient of the term is designed to bring out that the entity, as known to us, is devoid of any immediacy of its own (no immediacy like that of an actual entity in the process of its formation). The term "eternal" conveys the notion of something not, in its own material, settled as to any part of history. There is nothing in the

13

nature of an eternal object to indicate where, specifically, it is to be found exemplified.

There are many types of eternal objects: mathematical formulae, color, redness. Ultimate principles of metaphysics "bob up" everywhere. Particular eternal objects do not.

Every possibility is ultimately in the immediacy of some actuality. There must be a universal actuality (God).

The "accidental" side of eternal objects: the prehension of the eternal object "color" is the conceptual entertainment of a possibility (which may be actualized). Conceptual prehension is how a possibility exists as a factor in actuality. It is essential to note that actuality is not complete "matter of fact".

Possibilities do not just "stray about". How does the world bump into them? How do they enter into the world? Whitehead argues against Medieval Realism that every eternal object must (it is a metaphysical necessity) be entertained in actuality. The entertainment must be by conceptual prehension. Actuality must be described so as to account for this.

Whitehead then moved on to consider the venerable problem question: Are you going to divide reality into body and mind? He "remembered" that Aquinas would not have a complete division--mind is regarded as the form of the body.

Whitehead suggested that if you contrast body and mind, there are three ways of dealing with the problem of their relationship. One can deny the existence of "the other"--there is only matter, or there is only mind. (With some considerable vehemence Whitehead commented "Subjective Idealism is the mind humbugging itself".) "If you completely separate body and mind--it's an awful fudge getting them together."

He moved on to discuss "mentality": as you deal with large numbers of entities the importance of mentality fades. That is why people who deal with crowds realize you can neglect ultimate individual thoughts.

14

When you think frankly in the context of a civilization, you are in danger of knocking out its foundations. New, original thought is dangerous to society. Yet we must have complex novelty to support it against thought.

V

During the first part of May 1937 Whitehead delivered his last regularly scheduled lectures to Harvard students of Philosophy.

Most of the "main points" he made in the lectures of May 1, 4, 6, 8 are here reproduced in the following paragraphs. Many familiar themes reappear. The fact that he decided to stress them, at this point in his career, is surely significant.

With characteristic suspicion of over-simplification, Whitehead recommended that we should not exclude special experiences from philosophical consideration. Further, we should study the inconsistencies, as well as the consistencies, of great men. His strong interest in religions is reflected in a series of comments: There is no agreement in religious doctrine. We approach a region of "direct intuition". Religion is an individual matter. The great fallacy here as elsewhere is over-simplification.

Yet he claimed that all social orders are characterized by a certain dominant enthusiasm.

With this transition Whitehead made some remarks on social order, for example: the right of a social order to survive depends on the extent to which it contributes effectively to the higher social order of which it is a part. "Sooner or later the world overwhelms a social order--that is a general nuisance."

In a somewhat unusually vitriolic outburst, but not by any means unique, Whitehead said: "The learned tradition fails to recognize the transitory nature of a social order, because the learned tradition is not concerned with the truth, but rather with the learned adjustment of learned statements of antecedent learned people".

15

In this same general context, he suggested that Western philosophy is rooted in points of view of Mediterranean civilization of 2000 years ago (our knowledge is more widespread than theirs). We should not have too much respect for them.

Religion is one of the forces which enables us to transcend a provincial point of view. Religion must combine the characteristics of (a) peace, (b) stimulation. Each without the other is irreligious, --i.e., escapist tendency of a religion having only (a) and the orgiastic tendency of religions having only (b). The latter is the point of view of the modern world which began in Mesopotamia and ends in California.

In a rhetorical "aside" Whitehead remarked that evil is the cloud arising from opposing stimulations.

In a series of comments reminiscent of a famous passage in Process and Reality Whitehead outlined various notions of the religious factors in the universe. He offered the following classification (and remarked that we may use the term "God" to denote such factors):

(1) God is power--conceived in the guise of a dictatorial business manager--in any case an upper class notion;

(2) God is metaphysically "really real". In other words, God is envisaged as the total realization of all possibility. This God is a solipsist-- a complete God not concerned with the external world.

(3) God is love. His operative function is persuasion. This view of God is congenial to the "submerged" and exploited.

Whitehead paused to suggest that Christian theology during the first four centuries was an attempt, by a small group of intellectuals, to make Christianity respectable for the upper classes.

(4) God as the impersonal aspect of the world. This is the view of all Eastern theories of God, e.g., Buddhism.

5) God as "the mere fact of order". This is the
   God of "matter of fact" intellectuals. It is
   the 18th century "small town" view of the
   universe--which we cannot hold today.

n all these five notions there is an excluding of
:he historic process from God's nature. The teleo-
.ogical conceptions of the 18th century were mistaken.
'hey explained everything except the fact of disorder
n the universe.

6) God as the possibility of Emergent Order considered as the ideal at any given period.
   (S. Alexander.) God never actually is--rather
   is about to be.

7) God as unknowable (Spenser, Huxley).

8) All such speculation is beyond human capacity
   for thought.

   Whitehead claimed that in general there are
:hree sources of religion

   (a) masses of humanity

   (b) intellectuals

   (c) political myths

(is comments on genius are also worthy of note:
;enius is capacity for creative construction (some
:reation is evil). Genius is educated by criticism.

   Greatness depends on the fusion of criticism
and creation in art (in the broadest sense). Thus
:here is a Hegelian triad: Creation, Criticism, Art.

   Unless imagination can produce a picture of
vhat might be--creation is impossible.

   Knowledge is only important when it stimulates
:reative effort or is itself enjoyed in immediate
=eeling--where all values ultimately reside.

   The lecture of May 8, 1937 was composed of a
1umber of inter-related comments concerning philo-
;ophy. Whitehead began by stating that, in his
judgment, philosophy should "act as a mid-wife"--
>ring new ideas into being, i.e., seek to facilitate
:he function of reason.

17

There are two aspects of reason: (1) seeking new methods of practical action for promoting civilized society; (2) seeking new insights in order to understand the range of the universe. Each must be considered against the background of the whole of reality.

The universe is a strange mixture of permanence and transformation. Whitehead then proceeded to note that there are a number of dominant moods in philosophy (as it now exists):

1) Dogmatism - "I have definite knowledge. Everybody else is wrong"

2) Surprise - "I would not have suspected it.

3) Scepticism - vascillation between 1 and 2

4) Total disillusionment

This is the era of debunking, of escape from obligation by means of epigram.

Finally he remarked that there are two sorts (modes) of criticism in philosophy:

a) Compare thoughts with perceptions. The trouble with this empirical verification is that we can "cook our data".

b) Deductive reasoning--yet our premises are seldom, if ever, adequately stated.

VI

It is well to bear in mind the fact that the lectures Whitehead delivered at Harvard in the spring of 1937 were not his "final word" on philosophy.

During the academic year 1937-38 he gave a series of six lectures at Wellesley College. These were published as part of his Modes of Thought.

The form and content of these lectures are "not entirely surprising" to those who heard his Harvard lectures of 1936-37. They reflect many of the characteristics of "Whitehead as Lecturer" which have been described and illustrated in this chapter.

The Venerable Professor who, in 1936-37, was terminating his teaching career at Harvard, was famous as the author of The Aims of Education and other expositions of a well-developed educational philosophy. (See W.P.C. Chapter 5)

In discussing "Whitehead as Teacher" it is well to consider his avowed educational philosophy. At the beginning of the Preface of The Aims of Education he states: "The students are alive and the purpose of education is to stimulate and guide their self-development" (p. v).

More specifically--in Whitehead's judgment--students should be stimulated and guided so as to achieve culture and expert knowledge in some area of human endeavour. The "culture" he envisages is "activity of thought and receptiveness to beauty and humane feeling" (A.E. 1). A related corollary of this positive goal is: avoidance of passive reception of inert and disconnected ideas. In other words, an ideal education will produce persons whose ideas are dynamic sources of vigorous activity, and effective guidance, in the theoretical and practical affairs of life. Because the affairs of life are complex and inter-related, an efficient person must have a supply of ideas, which are inter-related and oriented to action, i.e., use. Worthy of note is Whitehead's statement: "What education has to impart is an intimate sense for the power of ideas, for the beauty of ideas, and for the structure of ideas, together with a particular body of knowledge which has particular reference to the life of the being possessing it" (A.E. 18).

This general outline of the characteristics of an ideal education is supplemented by a number of penetrating comments on University education. Of particular interest, for our purposes, is what he has to say about the faculty of a University.

Whitehead's basic position is that a university should present information in such a fashion that it is accepted and used imaginatively. As he aptly puts it: "A fact . . . is invested with all its possibilities it is no longer a burden on the memory: it is energizing as the poet of our dreams and, as the architect of purposes" (A.E. 139). This imagination should not be regarded as the opponent of careful factual observation, rather it is a way of illuminating facts.

It is obvious to Whitehead that if this ideal is to be actualized at a university, it must be exemplified by the faculty, particularly in their classroom activities, but also in other, general, behavior as well. In a series of brilliant phrases, Whitehead makes his conviction unmistakably clear. Professors must be "alive with living thoughts" (A.E. 1): "Wear their learning with imagination" (A.E. 145). Whitehead is above all anxious to "debunk" the pretentions of "know it all" dullards and pedants and those who are the "prima donnas" of University faculties. In his opinion a university professor should present himself as "an ignorant man thinking, actively utilizing his small share of knowledge" (A.E. 58).

A perceptive member of Whitehead's 1936-37 classes (lecture or tutorial) had no difficulty in recognizing the implementation of Whitehead's educational ideals in his performance as teacher. His obvious intellectual vitality, imaginative use of information, humility concerning his own activities, concern to achieve the solution of basic human problems both theoretical and practical--all aspects of his behavior as teacher--attest to the seriousness with which he devoted himself to his stated educational ideals. He achieved a very high level of approximation to these ideals on many, indeed most, occasions. It is of course true that any human being has times when he falls below his stated ideals and usual level of attainment. Whitehead's occasional "fall from grace" should not be regarded as standard behavior.

Note

A professor and his course are sometimes known and/or evaluated in terms of associated "suggested readings". Whitehead's "Cosmologies" course in 1936 involved the following list: Lucretius, On the Nature of Things--and extensive selections from: Plato, The Timaeus; C. Bailey, The Greek Atomists and Epicurus; Descartes, The Principles of Philosophy; L. Henderson, The Order of Nature and The Fitness of the Environment; G. Santayana, Some Turns of Thought in Modern Philosophy; and Whitehead's own Science and the Modern World, Process and Reality, Adventures of Ideas.

CHAPTER 2

WHITEHEAD AS TUTOR AND THESIS SUPERVISOR

Introduction

On registration day in the fall of 1936, approximately twenty graduate students in Philosophy at Harvard "lined up" beside the statue of Emerson in the hall which bears his name. One by one we entered a small seminar room and sought admission to Professor Alfred North Whitehead's "Philosophy 20."

Whitehead himself "sat in judgment." The student briefly outlined a project. If it was accepted a note was made in a little black book and Professor Whitehead set a time for the first session. He proposed to conduct the class as a tutorial, meeting each member for one hour a week in the study of his home.

My topic was, "Whitehead's theory of reality." It was accepted. A few days later I rang the bell at the Whitehead apartment in Radnor Hall. A maid in uniform appeared and conducted me into a large book-lined room where Professor Whitehead sat in a chair flanked by an adjustable writing desk.

Whitehead began this first session by making a number of apparently random comments in order to "break the ice," for example:

Philosophy is not a matter primarily of special disciplines, e.g., ethics. Yet there is an ethics of philosophical speculation.

We must deal with the question: Is a theory certain, a mere guess, or a working hypothesis?

Read Plato, Lucretius, Spinoza, Descartes, Hume, Leibnitz, Locke. Hume is most important for the reading of young philosophers.

Whitehead remarked that, in his intellectual development, he swung away from absolute idealism (Kant, Green, Caird) to a narrow form of analytic philosophy as practiced at Cambridge. He then attempted a synthesis: Specifically, there is an

21

emphasis on both permanence and process; a stress on the individuality of the really real, and on continuity. Any experience besides its immediacy gives an impression of something permanent underlying it. For example, (a) there is the immediate (passing) pleasure from a lump of sugar, and (b) the fact that the body must be kept going (permanence). In other words, there is a reference beyond the present moment.

I had come to Harvard hoping to clarify my understanding of Whitehead's theory of actual entities in general and his discussion of <u>eternal objects, objectification</u>, <u>God,</u> and <u>creativity in particular</u>.

When informed of this, he suggested that I prepare questions based on statements of (my interpretation of) his theories and offer criticisms set in the context of references to his texts. He further remarked: "Don't hesitate to criticize. There are contradictions. Mine is not a final and complete system."

All subsequent sessions followed the suggested pattern of "question and answer."

Specifically, at every meeting, I presented to him a typed "basis for discussion." Each was composed of several questions which were "set" in a series of background statements about, or quotations from, some phase of Whitehead's philosophy. These questions were of such a nature that it was hoped Whitehead would be able to answer: yes or no. In cases when, after careful examination of the "discussion" sheet, and some thought, he did so, I noted this fact on my carbon copy of the "basis for discussion." When he provided additional comment, I recorded it as accurately as possible after the end of the tutorial session.

What follows is a report of one graduate student's experience of Whitehead as teacher and philosopher. I have incorporated ("topics for discussion") questions exactly as I presented them to Professor Whitehead. His answers are recorded as he gave them.

In order to provide a simplified indication of Whitehead's approach to the topics discussed I have here revised the order in which I originally presented some of these questions.

22

Whitehead's Philosophical Position

Clarification of Whitehead's general philosophical position was obtained in the agreed fashion. (All discussion material which is prefaced by (J) and enclosed in quotation marks is a verbatim reproduction of what was before Whitehead in typed format as he answered a question and commented on the point at issue.)

(J) "C.W. Morris (Six Theories of Mind, pp. 183-84) contends 'Whitehead's course of procedure is to give a description of human experience . . . and then take this description as the key to the nature of reality ANY actual entity .' (A.I. 237) [1] Question-- Is this a correct statement?"

He commented that all we know about actual entities is directly derived from knowledge of our own experience (as an AE).* We know other AEs by objectification in our own experience. The body appears as an emotional welter of AEs in the same way and as the same sort of thing as the preceding AEs in the society of occasions constituting the ego,--only a little more vaguely.

In dealing with the external world, we have assumptions in which we put our trust. (1) We assume we are in touch with other things. We are mentally in touch. (2) Our bodies are physical objects among other physical objects. We know our bodies. Analogously, we know other bodies (objects).

When asked by Dewey: Are you a rationalist or an empiricist,[2] Whitehead replied that rationalism is needed to determine what system of abstractions is important--otherwise, you get a muddle-headed empiricism. Whitehead remarked also that Dewey's acceptance of Mead and his problem of the "past" is the pragmatic attempt to bring in rationalism. However, rationalism is not the basic factor. We must start with some insights. Rationalism then "cuts

---

*The abbreviation "AE" is frequently used in place of "actual entity."

their hair; washes their faces and fixes them up"
so as to be presentable in the available universe of
discourses. In particular, mystic insights are not
"damned nonsense." The nonsense comes in when
mystics claim no rational explication is possible.

(J) "Question--Is an examination of human
experience the source of your doctrine of the 'self-
creativity' of actual entities?"
Whitehead answered--"Yes."

(J) "Question--Am I correct in saying that you
use the term 'feeling' in several senses? It is
applied to (1) subjective form; (2) data; (3) a
complete actual entity?"
Whitehead answered--"Yes."

(J) "Question--When you say:--'Our developed
consciousness fastens on the sensum as datum; our
basic animal experience entertains it as a type of
subjective feeling'; (A.I. 315) do you mean, for
example, that a patch of red is a feeling? (not that
it is a nonaffective content which is felt?)"
Whitehead answered--"Yes."

Whitehead remarked that a patch of red is
derived from previous AEs. They are feelings. It
is a feeling (objectification). You analyze out of
a "red patchy" feeling--the red patch--that it is a
feeling just the same. Note apparent distinction
between feeling as act and feeling as content. When
we look at red, a natural feeling arises in response.
This is an art for art's sake situation. (See A.I.
315--Qualities qualify feelings, i.e., are feelings.)

Thus, for example, by green emotion (feeling)
Whitehead means that there are no abstract "sensa."
The patchiness of green is always a felt (in a certain
image) patchiness of green. In opposition to Hume, who
did not account for any relation of feeling to sensum,
Whitehead claims that there is always a normal relation. I feel the green patch either with pleasure
or disgust, (subjective form).

(J) "When you say that an actual entity is the
whole world present in one experience (I believe you
would say, in a sense, present at one spatiotemporal
locus) are you thinking in terms of the spread of an
energy discharge (which spreads all over the universe)
--to account for the availability to an actual

entity here, of an actual entity on the other side of the world? You would say, I think, that the actual entity from the other side of the world is available as data for the actual entity here, yet it can only be received into the being of the new actual entity, at its own discretion--by the process of objectification. This process is similar to emotional transfer (e.g., feeling of anger), from one occasion of my experience to another subsequent occasion.
Question--Is this a correct interpretation of your position?"
Whitehead answered--"Yes."

(J) "Your claim that an actual entity is a subject constituting itself by its feelings, would lead one fo suppose that you might be classed as a pansychist.
Question--Would you accept that interpretation?"
Whitehead replied that he is a panpsychist in the sense that every actual entity has a vague feeling of other AEs (as when you are waking up in the morning and become aware of other things). This is the only sense in which he is a panpsychist. He refuses to accept the theory that all things are of the nature of a "high class" soul, or self. He doesn't like to use   "awareness" instead of "prehension." It suggests "consciousness." This is what most panpsychists hold in his opinion.

Eternal Objects

A discussion of eternal objects was initiated by introducing typical general statements by Whitehead: Eternal objects are "Pure Potentials for the Specific Determination of Fact or Forms of Definiteness" (P.R. 32). "Any entity whose conceptual recognition does not involve a necessary reference to any definite actual entities of the temporal world is called an 'eternal object'" (P.R. 70; See also S.M.W. 221). "There are no novel eternal objects" (P.R. 33).

I then referred to some of his more specific statements: "'Sensa' constitute the lowest category of eternal objects" (P.R. 174); e.g., a definite shade of green (which can not be further analyzed).

"A color is eternal. . . . It comes and it goes.
. . . the same color." (S.M.W. 121) [3]

The designation of individual sensa as eternal
objects seemed to me to present serious difficulties
in view of many of Whitehead's statements, for
example, in P.R. 70: "By way of employing a term
devoid of misleading suggestions I use the phrase
'eternal object' for what. . . . I have termed a
'Platonic form': Any entity whose conceptual recognition does not involve a necessary reference to
any definite actual entities of the temporal world
is called an 'eternal object'". The point at issue
is, of course, this: Platonic forms are not the
data of sense, i.e., sensa. Sense data for Plato
are merely imitations of forms or participate in them.
Platonic forms as such are apprehended by intellect
(reason).

(J) I therefore enquired: "Do you accept Plato's
theory of Ideas, (Forms) as expressed in the earlier
dialogues, namely that Ideas, rationally apprehended,
are present in some way in objects of sensory apprehension, or to raise this issue in another way, isn't
it the case that things which are sensuously[4] appre-
hended--are not eternal objects but are only exemplifications of eternal objects? Please note that
these questions have to do with the ontological nature
of eternal objects. I am not, in these questions,
primarily concerned with epistemology. References to
modes of awareness, sensuous and intellectual are made
for the purpose of indicating more specifically the
types of entities to which I am referring.
Question ONE--Do you apply the term 'eternal object'
to those entities which are intellectually apprehended, e.g., triplicity? It is granted, of course,
that there is no purely intellectual apprehension. A
feeling tone (subjective form--a sensory experience)
and frequently an image (i.e., a sensuously apprehended
triangular patch) accompany an intellectual apprehension.
Question TWO--Do you, strictly speaking, intend to
apply the term 'eternal object' to those entities which
are sensuously apprehended, e.g., the triangular patch,
which is a particular exemplification of triplicity?
There is, of course, a certain subjective form operative
in this sensuous awareness of the triangular shape.

In a more simple fashion the issue is this:

Question--Would you call an EO* an essence (intellectually apprehended) and its exemplifications a concrete thing (sensuously apprehended)?"

Whitehead replied that an EO, as such, is an intellectually apprehended essence. A particular exemplification of it is sensuously apprehended. Hence sensuous apprehension of an eternal object as such is impossible. Thus, strictly (accurately) speaking, when he refers to a sensum as an eternal object he isn't really dealing with an eternal object as such. In other words, for example, we have intellectual apprehensions of triplicity, sensuous apprehensions of three fingers.

Whitehead pointed out, however, that he differs from Plato in one very important fashion. Plato's EOs (Ideas) are the ultimate reality. Further they have no essential concern with the world of particular things. Particular concrete things are only imitations. Whitehead's EOs are exemplified in actual entities. An AE is one exemplification of EOs because there is an inherent tendency for EOs to be exemplified in the actual world. Further AEs are just as real as EOs.

Speaking technically, we have a physical prehension of an EO as exemplified, i.e., an apprehension of a particular thing (sensuously apprehended). There is an intellectual grasp, i.e., conceptual prehension of an EO "as such." Other examples of EOs as such are: "an ideal League of Nations"; "How I am going to rearrange a room." Here we have EOs conceptually prehended--relatively free from accompanying images. In most cases, it is difficult to have a pure intellectual awareness of an EO as such, usually an image (exemplification of EO) appears also. (It is sensuously apprehended.) Imagination and memory provide many sensuously apprehended manifestations--also the external world, of course.

When questioned about his statement that there are "no novel EOs," Whitehead replied that he cannot see how we can create EOs.

I referred to D. Emmet's Whitehead's Philosophy of Organism. Whitehead remarked that Dorothy is a

*"EO" is used as an abbreviation for the term "eternal object."

27

"dear girl," but she blurs distinctions he tries to make. She gives a too Platonic picture of Whitehead. Whitehead, as an aside, stated that in epistemology one should center on common simple-minded experience. Hume is wrong in saying that all we can know is clear impressions. Too much modern epistemology has been concerned with saying exactly what is. It is not as simple as that.

In the course of the discussion I noted that an eternal object can only be understood by reference to (a) its peculiar and unique "individuality." (S.M.W. 222) An eternal object also has (b) a relational essence in that it has relations to (1) actual entities and (2) other eternal objects-- They are "internal relations." (S.M.W. 222) It is to be realized, however, that these so-called internal relations "do not involve the individual essences of the eternal objects." (S.M.W. 230) They constitute a perfectly general scheme of relationship which is the essence of any eternal object whatsoever.

Whitehead commented that if we try to consider an EO in absolute distinction and separation from all other EOs, we "assassinate it". An EO can't be completely conceptually prehended by an ordinary AE, i.e., all its implications (relational essence). All its interconnections with other EOs are only open to awareness in God's Primordial Nature, e.g., "blue." The line between "individual" and "relational" essence can be drawn in a hard and fast fashion.

I next raised the question as to how an eternal object is exemplified.

(J) "Question--Just what is your treatment of the process by which an essence is exemplified in the actual entity?" Whitehead replied that he has no particular description beyond the fact that the EO "greenness" becomes exemplified as a (feeling of greenness or) "green feeling." It is a matter of fact and that's all there is to it. This is what logical positivists should mean when they talk about tautologies, but they don't.

Whitehead commented further that there might conceivably be exact reproduction of the same EO in different AEs. Yet it would be differentiated by the where element (i.e., physical prehensions of something

pecifically there here). Conceptual prehensions
on't give a where (i.e., EOs are not confined to
ne particular AE) but they give whereness in the
ense that there is a definite AE having a conceptual prehension. Plato's EOs are "abstract."
here is no relational essence, i.e., there is no
eference to other EOs, or the external world. They
re static and lifeless.

Whitehead pointed out that he believes EOs are
in the bosom of reality" (actuality). The basic
nterest, in part, has been to show EOs (Ideas) are
nvolved in particular things. Whitehead wants to
how that EOs are a basic part of actuality: They
ave necessary relations and a drive toward reali-
ation. In this sense, it is possible to speak of
eleology in the universe. EOs are both historic
nd eternal. And as "exemplifications," they are
nduring in God as Consequent.

Another topic was introduced thus: (J) "You
tate: 'All actual entities are positively prehended;
ut only a selection of eternal objects is posi-
ively prehended '. (See P.R. 66, 79.) It may
ppear that there is a problem here: How is it pos-
ible to feel an eternal object and then reject it?
oesn't the mere act of feeling the eternal object
ake it a part of the new entity? However, an
rgument of this sort overlooks the complexity of the
rehensive process. The difficulty can be met by
eference to the distinctions between 'initial data'
the world as it presents itself) and 'objective data'
the content selected for use in the new actual entity)
P.R. 337-8). Thus, the mere fact of feeling data
initial data) doesn't thereby constitute them a com-
onent of the actual entity. Having been viewed, a
atum may be eliminated. Question--Is this a correct
nterpretation of the reply you would make to such a
riticism?" Whitehead's answer: "Absolutely correct
though not quite satisfied with my [Whitehead's]
wn position here)."

Whitehead remarked further that the nature of
egative prehensions is illustrated by the experience
f an artist. He produces his work by the exclusion
f unseasonable (unseemly) possible patches of red,
tc. The decisions of the artist becomes more and
ore specialized as it goes on. The art of excluding
oncrete materials not required is a basic part of the
rocess.

Whitehead also made the very significant comment that his theory of EOs is concerned with the problem of getting stability and absoluteness in the universe. Nevertheless eternal objects have, for the most part, accidental relation to particular world events. It is, however, true that some EOs, e.g., "creativity" and "causation," are exemplified in all AEs, while others such as "blue" are not. In a sense it may be necessary to claim that some EOs are more eternal than others.

Somewhat ruefully Whitehead remarked that he can't see how Hartshorne and others get along without EOs. It is evident that a quality exemplified at one place can be exemplified at another. This can only be stated in terms of EOs. In his (Whitehead's) theory there is no problem of EOs cut off from concrete realities--or denying reality to concrete things.

Objectification

The discussion of objectification was initiated by referring to two apparently different approaches by Whitehead to this topic. It was noted that he remarks in general terms: "Each actuality is prehended by means of some element of its own definiteness." (P.R. 230) Then he more specifically stated (a) that data consist of phases of actual entities directly "appropriated" (P.R. 246) having been "transferred" (P.R. 364), "emotional forms transmitted from occasion to occasion" (P.R. 174). There is also a reference to the "subjective form" being continuous throughout the successive moments of experience. (A.I. 235) On the other hand (b) there are references to the "two way, i.e., relational functioning" of eternal objects (P.R. 249. See also 446) which seem to indicate that objectification involves only the presence of the one eternal object in different actual entities.

Therefore the question was asked: (J) "What, exactly, takes place in the process whereby one actual entity is objectified in another? Is it a case of, for example, (a) a particular patch of green (exemplification of the eternal object 'green') handed on from one actual entity to another; or (b) Is it a case of one eternal object (essence) being exemplified in two

distinct AEs, there being no transfer of content from
one actual entity to another. --Alternative (a) seems
to be that which you usually hold." Whitehead answered
--"You are correct, I hold the first position. But it
is an inadequate and vague way of expressing an insight
which is difficult to verbally express in its complete
details."

In a further comment he emphasized that he had
great trouble in expressing the details of his insights.
The mystical experiences of Wordsworth and Shelley
(brooding presence of nature) are typical of objectification. Also these are things beyond ourselves yet
in us, e.g., Dictates of the Supreme Court (beyond),
yet they are present in our awareness of them. The
best example of conformation or continuity of feeling
(besides that of Wordsworth's experience of the presence
of nature) is that of the successive occasions of our
own experience (as a self) or the relation of self to
body. We experience ourselves as a unity and also as a
successive society of "events." Each event takes content from the preceding one and absorbs it into its
own being. The content as such is handed on from one
to the other.

Whitehead was anxious to emphasize that in general,
the problem of objectification is a problem of causation.
There is no causation in the old sense of separate and
distinct substances having accidental interaction.
Causation (revised sense) is a genuine process of self-
creation by mutual interaction. The old usage of the
term is the only one recognized by most philosophers.
Whitehead means by prehension, "causation" in the
revised sense. He made special reference to Process
and Reality, p. 31-2, paragraph 4 and to page 92, paragraph 2, and the last line of paragraph 1. Whitehead
objected to the Aristotelian "primary substance" for
the reason that it is "just here." It has no connections with anything else. Hume in his Treatise is
a dogmatic empiricist. He refuses to note relations;
is concerned only with a complete atomism of sensa.
However, in the Dialogues on Natural Religion, Hume
accepts a position like that of James in Radical
Empiricism. He stresses all the factors we are aware
of in our experience avoiding the extreme "Pragmatic"
implications which James worked out: justification of
belief--reference to the future .

In characteristic fashion Whitehead reiterated a
favorite theme, namely: Only what is clearly and

distinctly conceived (or perceived) is verbalized.
Frequently, however, that which is verbalized is
superficial. Abstractions taken as self-existent--
having no concourse with other things or entities--
are most dangerous (Plato and Aristotle).

In order to avoid any possible misunderstanding
and to "double check" Whitehead's view on the place of
eternal objects in objectification, further questions
on several different occasions were asked as follows:

(J) "Question--By your doctrine of the 'two-way
function' of eternal objects (P.R. 249; 364) do you
mean: (1) that the same eternal object (essence) is
exemplified in several numerically distinct actual
entities; or (2) a numerically identical exemplification of an eternal object (essence) is at one moment
in one actual entity and at the next moment in a succeeding actual entity?"
Whitehead replied that in talking about two-way
function of eternal objects, he is concerned with
"conformations" of feelings. In virtue of the process of objectification, the same EO appears in two
AEs. The real connection between AEs is not due to
the fact of the presence of the same EO in the two AEs
but due primarily to transfer of "concrete content."

I further suggested: (J) "Your statement that
'the solidarity of the universe is based on the relational functions of eternal objects' (P.R. 249)[5]
(Solidarity having previously been accounted for in
terms of objectification, P.R. 10) leads me to believe
that, when you refer to the 'two-way function of eternal objects,' you are referring to objectification,
i.e., the process by which actual concrete relationships are forged. It is, of course, true that in the
actual entities thus related by objectification, the
same eternal object is exemplified. Question--Is this
all you mean by the relational function of the eternal
objects?"
Whitehead answered-- "Yes."

(J) "Question--When you say: 'The percipient
prehends the nexus of contemporary occasions by the
mediation of eternal objects, which it inherits from
its own past"--don't you mean exemplifications of
eternal objects from its own past, rather than mere
eternal objects (essences) as such. (It is, of course,

rue that these exemplifications embody essences, i.e.,
eternal objects ; in this sense eternal objects are
nherited). Is this a correct interpretation of your
osition?"
"hitehead replied: "Accepted as expounded."

Whitehead's theory of objectification obviously
oes not involve an elimination of the need for eternal
bjects. It was pointed out that (J) "various critics[6]
ave stated that in earlier books you account for
dentity, permanence, universality, abstraction, and
otentiality by reference to eternal objects. In later
orks, you appeal to the objectification of actual
ntities to explain these factors. It is concluded
hat you have either contradicted yourself, or no longer
eed eternal objects. Question--Would your reply be
hat, for example, identity manifest by an eternal ob-
ect is different from that manifest (or exemplified) by
 personal society of actual entities. That is to say,
he essence 'identity' is exemplified in two different
ypes of entity--eternal objects and actual entities.
t is then absurd to say that, because actual entities
xemplify identity, therefore eternal objects aren't
equired as exemplifications of it. Question--Is this
 correct conjecture of your answer?" Whitehead
nswered: --"Accepted as expounded."

In general, Whitehead is concerned to develop a
etaphysics, in opposition to Leibnitz, in which en-
ities have "windows." This is accounted for by the
loctrine of prehensions--"the prehensions are the
indows."

It is to be noted that in Whitehead's theory of
bjectification there is not an (a) exact or (b)
omplete transference of "material" (content) from an
ld to the new actual entity. (P.R. 80) These topics
ere introduced as the basis for discussion in the
ollowing fashion: (J) "(a) 'The cause passes on its
eeling to be reproduced by the new subject as its own.
. . But the reinaction is not perfect.' (P.R. 362-3)
ertain 'inhibitions or additions, weakenings or in-
ensifications, (appear) due to the history of its
roduction.' (P.R. 362) (b) Only some feelings are
ransferred in the process of objectification. Other
eelings in the original actual entities are dis-
issed, eliminated from the new actual entity." (See:
.R. 321, A.I. 256)

Whitehead commented that since any AE takes content from all others (theoretically at least; in any case in varying degrees), there must be limitations in the contributions made by various AEs. (Otherwise, all AEs would be incarnations of God.) He was certain that the above principle must hold; but it is not clear on details. However, there are hints available: In science, there are "forces going this way and that," but one can, for practical purposes, deal with this situation in terms of a parallelogram of forces, i.e., by a process of simplifications--"eliminating extremes of difference." The Second Law of Thermodynamics is another illustration--force "runs down." Aesthetic and moral experience illustrate acceptance and rejection; i.e., it is a fact of life. Further, in our relation to some "things" spatiotemporal facts are irrelevant, e.g., in the interchange of ideas between A.N.W. and A.H.J. the positions of their bodies and time elapsed are irrelevant. This fact of an objective order of things apart from our flux of experience is a fact of life. Offering another example of negative prehension, Whitehead remarked "I feel that what I am excludes other things (i.e., characteristics). I am a good citizen, not a bad one. That is present before me as a distinct characteristic. Evil tendencies are not present, clearly delineated." We are aware of a vague background of excluded possibilities. However, Whitehead was not completely satisfied with his description of this phenomenon. In general, objectification is the process made possible by negative prehensions, i.e., the inclusion of objectified data, as contrasted with "initial data."

Turning to more general considerations I raised what appears to be a fundamental issue.

(J) "It seems to me that, in a sense, your metaphysical position implies that an actual entity is restricted to the experience of its own component elements. It is true that the data which an actual entity receives, come from other actual entities. Yet as experienced, these data are part of the constituent content of the prehending actual entity. They do not now belong to the original source since the actual entity which provides data must pass out of existence before these data are made available. This line of approach, which culminates in your theory that an actual entity never has direct experience of the contemporary world seems contrary to your emphasis on the direct mutual interrelations of actual entities. Question--Did you intend to allow, in the sense noted above (and only in this sense), that an actual entity is restricted to the experience of its own component elements? (Note: I am concerned with the status of the data experienced, not with the use which it might be put to, as in the symbolic reference involving presentational immediacy.)" Whitehead answered: "There is a danger here. I haven't been careful in formulating my ideas."

Considering the same general problem, it was pointed out that (J) "your usual statement of the doctrine of objectification is to the effect that an actual entity does not provide data for a new actual entity until it (the first actual entity) has 'died.' 'Data' are available only after the internal existence of the actual entity 'has evaporated, worn out and satisfied.' (P.R. 336) The superject is not of the substance of the subject. (See P.R. 129) When you say:--An actual entity 'at any stage . . . is subject--superject' (374) you don't mean to say that at any stage in the development of an actual entity data are available, do you?" Whitehead answered: "No."

(J) "Question--Is one reason why 'contemporary actual entities' don't interact the fact that they are not yet complete and therefore can't provide data? This is in addition to the fact that actual entities must be in the relationship of temporal sequence if there is to be direct objectification of one in the other." Whitehead answered: "Yes."

I also stated: (J) "In view of the fact that actual entities are either coming to be or passing away--never really are (as such), isn't it very easy to slip into inaccurate expressions? When it is said, for example, that actual entity 'A', prehends actual entity 'B', one gets the impression that two more or less exactly determinate entities are in interaction. Yet, as a matter of fact, 'A' is not yet and 'B' has passed on. It apparently comes to this: At no moment can you say 'here' is an actual entity, complete and determinate. All you have are processes of growth toward 'actual entityhood' (and the demise of actual entities). In a sense you don't have an actual entity as such because you never catch one complete. It is either coming or going--never 'here.'

35

Question--Is this a fair statement or do you hold
that for a 'split second' the complete actual entity
pauses to enjoy itself as fully complete--before
passing on?"
Whitehead answered: "Yes it is a fair statement. I
do not accept the alternative."

Another general problem was then introduced
thus: (J) "I judge that while in one sense an actual
entity can not be thought of as confined to one particular position in the universe; yet in a perfectly
definite sense it can be said to have a specific
locus. The problem arises, as to how content is
transferred from one actual entity to another, distant
(in the common sense meaning) from it. I judge that
you refer to intermediary actual entities, which do
the "handing on" (as in a "personal" series, or
society); or that you would use the analogy of an
electrical discharge which spreads out from its center.
Question--Is this a correct interpretation?"
Whitehead answered: "Yes and no."

He explained his answer by stating that the problem of transfer of content is correctly interpreted
if we are talking about lower elements of things,
i.e., physical prehensions, of things described in
spatiotemporal terms. Here there is transference by
contact. Basic emotions are transferred from one AE
to an adjacent one. With reference to those higher
qualities of life (conceptually prehended) where
spatiotemporal relation does not apply, we have direct
relationship but it is not a matter of transference in
the "physical" sense. In vocal intercourse, i.e., the
series of squeals, physical transference of content,
drops out of focus and there is direct spiritual intercourse between AEs which are not in close-knit serial
sequences. A form of telepathy (mental intercourse
with little or no physical basis) is normal in conversation and other less common experience. Generally
speaking, we can say that, on lower levels of existence, intercourse is by transference of concrete
content, on higher levels, directly across gaps (i.e.,
a concrete medium is not involved). It is possible
that there may be intermixture of methods. This telepathy must be checked by a rational metaphysics, otherwise, there is madness.

The preceding discussion formed the basis for a
reference to Whitehead's theory of perception. He

36

remarked that the perception of a book is not in the
mode of causal efficacy, i.e., immediately felt transfer of feeling. It is presentational immediacy. In
seeing a pencil, you are not aware of transfer of
feeling from the pencil to your "presiding occasion"
(mind). In reality, you use feeling derived from
your immediate bodily state to apply to the contemporary world. ("You embroider the data. . . .") Of
course, the feeling you take from your bodily state
is ultimately derivative from the "past" components
of the contemporary world (which you assume carries
on the same characteristics). The fact that the
feelings (sense data) you are aware of are derived
from the body is proved by the fact that we are aware
that we see with our eyes (physiological organism)--
(not that these feelings are derived from the external
world). "This is described in the Category of Transmutation). We always have a "sense" that our experience may be delusive. One wonders if the field
is really green.

In perception, since it is superficial, we only
select some aspects of an object--overlook others.
We have an inaccurate opinion of how a thing looks--
disregard details. In presentational immediacy, we
overlook the "conditioning factors" of causal efficacy.
It is a case of which important aspect of common, ordinary sense experience we will use, i.e., (1) direct
awareness of the outer world or (2) (a) regard the
body as source of data, but (b) remain uncertain of
correctness."

Religion and God--General Comments

From time to time Whitehead interjected comments
concerning religion in general and views of God in
particular. These comments are here gathered together
and introduced as a background for his more technical
discussions of God.

Whitehead stated that he wanted to formulate a
philosophy of religion which will do justice to "the
inner spiritual experiences of the race." The religion
of the Gospels is basic but "high-grade intellectual

swells" like Augustine and Aquinas corrupted it.
"Man is a queer combination of delicacy of spirit
with a brutality which would disgrace rats." Yet,
in it all, there is manifest a drive to a higher
type of existence. Religion would profit if it included a mixture of Buddhism, a sense of duty and
Confucianism.

Whitehead admitted that he did not get all his
insights adequately organized in his idea of God. In
any case he wasn't primarily interested in God: "Just
brought him in to show he belonged." But God does
belong and hence Whitehead is opposed to those who
would "save" religion by eliminating essential
features. This was his opinion of the Humanistic
approach.

Whitehead was most vehement in his opposition to
the idea that God is like an oriental despot. He
told a story about a student reading an essay to an
Oxford don. The young man solemnly intoned: "Before
God we must be abject-abject." The old scholar burst
out: "Tut, tut; no, no--not abject; respectful,
respectful."[7]

Continuing his criticisms of the work of "dis-
torting theologians" Whitehead stated that a static
and complete God can have absolutely nothing to do
with contingency. Gilson's book, The Spirit of
Mediaeval Philosophy, brings Hume's Demea back on the
stage. Aristotle's God can only be conceptually related to human affairs. A completely real God can
never create. If he attempts to at all, there is a
world of mere appearance. No real individual human
experience is possible. The God of the mediaeval
world was the only creature.

We should construct our notion of the nature of
God by reference to our knowledge of what we experience.

Whitehead is trying to say that God is actual--
yet actual in a different sense from ordinary AEs.
How different? Well, different in some understandable
sense. You start with your own experience. You experience yourself as an actuality. This is the only
datum you have. God must be described in these terms.
Gilson et al try to describe God in terms of concepts
which are not understandable, i.e., have no reference
to ordinary experience. We have no experience of

perfect and necessary Being. Gilson is like Demea
with his "appeal to ignorance." Cleanthes and Philo
can't quite answer the question.

In the context of this discourse Whitehead
remarked that the Christian God is a "ferocious
finite entity." He (Whitehead) strives to strike a
mean between Christianity and Buddhism. This comment "sparked" the following question, (J) "Will you
please enlarge on this suggestion?"

Whitehead replied that the traditional expression of ideas about God has been characterized by
absurd exaggerations. (1) The "Reality" of God
has been stressed at the expense of the limited (or
none at all) reality of finite AEs. (It is true
that God is different.) (2) They exaggerate his
"Personality." Here Buddhism is saner in being
satisfied with vaguer notions. In some Christian
thought God is made a rather barbaric ferocious,
vain, creature who rejoices in the reception of
ridiculous compliments. Whitehead said if anyone
came to him and plied him with those compliments,
he'd "give the idiot a good kick." But Buddhism
whittles away the personality of God too much.
"Personality" is a very difficult sort of thing to
get hold of. There is: (1) immediacy (myself now);
also (2) objective immortality of an antecedent
society, i.e., self in the past. Personality is a
line of dominant inheritance. When do you become a
personality? Is it the first wiggle in your mother's
womb?, or the first time you think? Thus when you
say God is an actual personality, you are using a
very vague concept.

In the midst of this serious discussion Whitehead embarked on a facetious digression to the effect
that the philosophies of East and West are partially
explicable in terms of devotion to opium on the one
hand and wine, beer and spirits on the other.

The abdication of Edward the VIII was at this
time very much before the American public. Apropos
of this Whitehead referred to "that German family--
that head of hair. Once we thought it a bond of
unity. Now we realize it is a symbol of a bond."[8]

God as Primordial

The discussion turned to an examination of
Whitehead's technical theory of God. After an
introductory statement: (J) "God is an actual
entity," I asked: "By God's primordial nature you
mean his conceptual prehensions; by his consequent
nature you mean his physical prehensions--don't you?"
Whitehead answered: "Yes."

He then commented that God's primordial nature
is not included among the Categoreal notions, yet
it should have been. In order to answer the question--
"where does novelty come from," the Category of
Conceptual Reversion (V) is introduced. Later, when
God's P nature ("P" is an abbreviation for the term
"primordial") is discussed, this category may be dis-
pensed with." Whitehead stated that this category
is not as coherent as the others. Category VI, for
example, explains a phase of "Creative Synthesis."
Category V does not. More specifically, the doctrine
of Conceptual Reversion which was introduced to account for novelty (i.e., there is a collection of
EOs in relevant relationship) implies that either
(a) EOs stray about the universe on their own--no
way of interaction--"fluke in" from nowhere, or (b)
there is an AE (God) in which the EOs are functioning.
Whitehead admitted that he should have introduced
God's P nature sooner.

The problem of "stability" and "absoluteness"
is complicated (by Whitehead) when he says that
God's P nature is accidental. It is one organization
of EOs. Might not an other organization be possible?
Yet after all, the present organization is all we
have. It is to be accepted--the "ultimate irratio-
nality."

Whitehead emphasized that God as P. has an
aspiration to enter into history. He is both con-
structive and destructive, i.e., is concerned to get
rid of repetition, and to have new orders and entities
built up. Speaking technically, in God as P there is
an appetition to realize EOs in the world. (NB--Appe-
tition is a subjective form, the opposite of disgust.)

But God as P is not the only or basic source (cause) of what happens in the world. If this were so, (1) our everyday decisions would make no difference, (2) moral decisions would be meaningless. While all EOs are present to God's P nature as possibilities, God cannot tell what particular events will ulti- mately happen because each actual entity is "self- creating" (using, of course, available materials). When events happen, he can tell the "logical" conse- quences. Consider an illustration of the importance of "sporadic" events. Two young people (Mrs. Simpson and King Edward VIII) of 42 meet. That may change the whole course of history.

Two students were in Whitehead's study, one going and the other coming. He remarked: "Let me give you 'young things' a bit of advice--always answer your letters and keep your desk tidy." Whitehead admitted that he does not write letters because they "break up" his concentration.

The discussion shifted to an examination of one of Whitehead's most famous phrases. I asked: (J) "When you say that God is the 'Principle of Con- cretion' (P.R. 374) do you mean, more specifically, that God provides a 'pattern' (eternal object) which a new actual entity accepts as its subjective aim and uses as a guide in its processes of concretion? In this sense God provides, not is, the Principle of Concretion. My problem is this: Is it wise to call an actual entity a 'principle?' (It is true that an actual entity is the exemplification of a principle.) Isn't a principle, as such, an eternal object?" Whitehead replied: "You are right." God is not a principle. A principle is an EO (i.e., a possibility) while God is an actuality. Whitehead commented that his language was vague in Religion in the Making. It gave him good publicity but is not the best intro- duction to his philosophy. He likes the first two chapters.

It was emphasized that while all possibilities (EOs) as such are present in God's nature, i.e., are intellectually apprehended (conceptually prehended), any exemplifications are not present in God's P nature but in his consequent nature. God as P is not one entity. God as P and C ("C" is an abbreviation for the term "Consequent.") is one entity. Whitehead

admitted that he "wobbled" on that point. At one
time in Process and Reality he did almost suggest
that God as P might be a separate kind of AE. The
principle of concretion when exemplified in God
results in the maximum of vividness and the minimum of distortion. The experiences of the King,
Baldwin and Archbishop[9] are all experienced in God
as a tragedy. They are all there--in their proper
perspective.

God's Consequent Nature

The preceding brief references to God's consequent nature led to further discussion of this topic.
Whitehead contended that the various AEs do not retain
their individuality as such; but the distinctness of
elements (phases) of these AEs are immortal in God's
C nature. Whitehead's notion of God's C nature is,
in this sense, pantheistic. In God's C nature, the
distinctiveness of AEs, in the temporal world, is
lost. But elements which were in our experience are
more vivid in God's i.e., he evaluates them more
accurately. His experience is richer. The individuality of elements in our experience is enhanced in
God. This is what Whitehead means by immortality.

Probing further into the topic I said: (J) "I
judge that when you refer to God retaining immediacy
(P. R. 530) the 'immediacy' God 'retains' is his own,
not that of actual entities objectified in him. Some
phases of their being are eliminated as they pass
into God. When you say 'nothing is lost,' don't you
mean that in God (as Consequent) actual entities are
transformed. Nothing is lost which can be saved'
(i.e., is worthy of being saved.)" In reply Whitehead commented that God's immediacy doesn't "die."
There is no elimination in God's nature as such.
There is, of course, elimination of some of the data
presented for inclusion in God's nature. God's C
nature is conditioned by data from the developing
actual world. He can foresee all future possibilities
but not what exactly the future will be. Whitehead
explained that God's C nature is introduced to deal
with moral and aesthetic problems. Further, God as
C accounts for experience of objective succession
of the external world. In our own experience we have
a "specious present" yet there is only quasiobjective

immortality. We cannot measure (stand off and observe) our successive stages of self creation. We are always enmeshed in subjective immediacy. The "external" world must be regarded as separate from "my" intrinsic self-creation process.

A related issue was then introduced. I pointed out: (J) "You refer to the everlasting nature of God, which is in a sense, non-temporal and in another sense temporal. (See: P.R. 524-33) Question--In what sense is God temporal?" Whitehead replied that by "temporal" he here means "growth," not rising and passing away. He stated that God grows, and thus in a sense is historical. God is everywhere (in time). God is not historical in the sense of "whereness" or as a merely "present" who fades.

In a typical "historical aside" Whitehead denounced the complete disjunction of substances, the only relation being "a quality of." He remarked that Bradley in Essays on Truth and Reality, e.g., in "Immediate Experience" notes the reality of connections, while continuing to say with Aristotle that a substance cannot have real connections, contends that a concrete universal can. Bradley's doctrine of the concrete universal is just a "fudge" to save himself from saying that Aristotle is wrong.

God: An Actual Entity

In a sense the preceding discussion of God's primordial nature and God's consequent nature verge on artificial abstraction. Unfortunately some of Whitehead's own published statements have laid the foundation for a misunderstanding of his actual view concerning God.

He has seen fit to discuss the "natures" of God separately. By a distinction of reason, God is first considered in the abstraction of a primordial actuality. It is unfortunate, that on occasion Whitehead suggests that these "factors in God," "deficient in actuality," are as a matter of fact actualities in their own right.

When I presented this comment to Whitehead in the context of my thesis he wrote in the margin: "A great carelessness on my part."[10]

More specifically in a subsequent paragraph I
wrote: "The statement that God as consequent is
'fully actual' (P.R. 524) is not exactly correct.
What Whitehead apparently means is that, because God,
the actual entity, has a physical pole (consequent
nature) he is fully actual. (Not that the physical
pole, as such, isn't fully actual since actualities must
have both poles.) This same general criticism applies
to the statement that God as consequent is conscious
(P.R. 524). In reality God is conscious when he has
both physical and mental poles, so that fact, present
by physical prehension, can be confronted by alternatives (conceptual prehensions). In short, the mere
presence of a physical pole as such does not render
God conscious."

Here again Whitehead appended a marginal note:
"You are quite right here."[11] In brief, God is an
actual entity of which those natures are constituent
and interrelated ingredients. In view of this fact
the rest of the discussion dealt with the full complexity of God.

Whitehead remarked that God's P nature is prior,
but not temporally. His P nature finds history and
every fact of history finds the P nature of God. God's
C nature is influenced by (i.e., its formation is controlled by) God's P nature, also, by individual decisions of other AEs. In God as consequent (as noted
previously) there is both historic perishing of other
AEs and real immortality. Some of the "historic"
past is lost. There is real "passing out," e.g., the
details of our own past experience are not all retained
in God. But the "past" elements in God's nature are
never lost. These comments provide the necessary background for a discussion of tragedy in God's experience.
There is always elimination when things are objectified
in God. That is the tragedy which even God does not
escape. A perfectly satisfied God is damnable. God
experiences evil as tragedy. God is tragic and noble,
not perfect. In God, evil does not lose its character.
It is not ultimately a neutral element in an all-
inclusive perfection (as in Absolute Idealism).

Whitehead remarked that in the last part of
Process, he was not clear on what he wanted to say.
In the last chapter of Adventures ("Peace"), God's
effect on the world is dealt with in terms of peace
and the individuality of God is lost sight of. He

hopes to bring these two chapters together. In a genuine sense, there is objectification of what is worthy--in God, yet he is forced to leave out much. Further, things in God are transmuted and transformed.

Whitehead then proceeded to expound the meaning of several key phrases. Concerning Process and Reality, p. 526, line 5, he stated that in: God "is poet of the world," the word "poet" was employed in the sense of its Greek root "maker." In the phrase: "with 'tender patience leading' it, persuading it," the reference to "tender patience" shows that he has the "pluck" to go to experience which is deepest and most profound to get his insights. He relies on the total wealth of human experience. With reference to Process and Reality, p. 525, last line: "God's role is not the combat of productive force with productive force,"-- he pointed out that this does not mean that God has no efficient power. His superject nature gives as efficient causation as any other A.E. But it is causation from such a high point of view and of such general scope as to harmonize the whole. It does not have the character of short-time combat, limitation of aim, that is to say, combat of force with force as in the case when you are confronted by a madman. Then you forget about the choir of heaven and the internal gyrations of the atom and concentrate on the immediate activity (limited in scope of interest) of subduing the madman.

Whitehead contended that the proper notion of "power" is like that discovered in the "British Constitutional" setup,--the King, Prime Minister, voters, do not have absolute power. At the best, they can only be vividly persuasive.

This remark led me to ask the following question: (J) "Is it correct to say that God exerts only as much causal influence on the world as any other actual entity,--i.e., by providing 'data' for other actual entities but not forcing data on them."

Whitehead replied that God does not force data of any sort on other actual entities. However, God has more causal influence than other AEs in the sense that he continues, while others pass away. He added, as an aside, that Part III should come before Part II in Process and Reality (though not quite sure).

In general Whitehead contended that his view of God has more richness of content than Buddhism's Nirvana. His Philosophy of Religion might be called an effort to "true up" Nirvana.

In answer to a question Whitehead stated that H.N. Wieman "starts off admirably, but, finally, being in an intellectual funk, divests it of all meaning.[12] Wieman reduces religion to a matter of creative inter-action--social satisfaction."

Whitehead pointed out that Religion in the Making "takes a kick" at the liberal theologians of the 19th century. The universe is complex. They make it too simple. Whitehead considered his Religion in the Making was a complete failure. Yet it has proved one of his most successful works.

The discussion then turned to a consideration of more technical aspects of Whitehead's theory of God. I pointed out that in a sense every actual entity has a definite locus. The question then arose: "Is it possible to indicate God's locus?"

In reply Whitehead stated that in respect to the world, God is everywhere. Yet he is a distinct entity. The world (events in it) has a (specific) locus with reference to him, but he has no locus with reference to the world. This is the basis of the distinction between finite and infinite. God and the world have the same locus. It is a matter of emphasis which you pick out as occupying the locus. He does not want to set God over against the other AEs, as AEs are (for practical purposes) located at specific (separate) loci with reference to each other.

In answer to my question: (J) "Can you think of God (as C) as a 'society'?" Whitehead replied that he had considered the possibility, i.e., a society is what endures; an AE passes away. But, said Whitehead, "The answer is no." In a society the past is lost (i.e., one ordinary AE fades away and only some of its data are passed on to another AE. But, in God, his past is not lost. Yet, in a sense, God is a society (this Whitehead has not thought out), AEs passing into God as C provide a group (society) of distinguishable components though the AEs as such do not survive.

I next introduced a basic criticism. (J) Question--"Does not your description of God make it difficult for you to say that God is an actual entity in the usual sense of the term? For example, 'an actual entity has perished when it is complete,' (P.R. 126) as contrasted with: God retains immediacy and creative advance (P.R. 524), i.e., is never complete in the sense that he 'perishes.'" Whitehead answered: "Yes."

(J) Question--"If God never 'perishes,' how can he provide data for other actual entities? Data are only available after the 'internal existence' of the actual entity 'has evaporated.'" (P.R. 336). Whitehead replied: "This is a genuine problem. I have not attempted to solve it."

(J) Question: "Am I correct in assuming that for the purposes of your metaphysics, you hold that the metaphysical situation has always been as it is now; namely: actual entities interacting creatively; eternal objects; God, with his primordial, consequent and superject natures? The fact that you discuss God's consequent and superject natures at the end of Process and Reality does not indicate that God had only his primordial nature for a long time; nor do you hold that his consequent nature came into being only after the world of ordinary actual entities appeared, with the help of God's primordial nature, which came first. Question: Is this a correct interpretation of your position?"

Whitehead answered: "Yes" and commented that there is no sense in talking about a "beginning" of the universe. There is no temporal sequence of the sort: Process (creativity); God as P; God as C, in that order of appearance.

Creativity

There was considerable discussion of Whitehead's concept of "Creativity" with particular reference to points made in D. Bidney's "Spinoza and Whitehead," The Philosophical Review, November 1936.[13] (See pp. 106-11)

I introduced the topic by saying: (J) "As I understand it, you use the term 'creativity' to refer to the

47

fact that a new actual entity arises by appropriating data provided by other actual entities, i.e., creativity is a process of interrelations between actual entities. There is no actual 'creativity' apart from actual entities (i.e., actual entities in process of self-origination). (A.I. 303; 230)   It is therefore evident that, when you use the term 'creativity,' you do not, strictly speaking, refer to some stuff, reality, substratum, entity, from which actual entities emerge by a process of individualization. (S.M.W. 247-8; P.R. 10)   Question--Is this a correct interpretation of your use of the term 'creativity'?"

Whitehead answered: "Yes" (broadly), and commented that every element of the universe is present in any AE. (Therefore, creativity is.) The character "creativity" is nothing apart from a fact (AE)-- which is the entire universe then. (See P.R. 31)

I continued and said: (J) "You refer to 'creativity' as the 'universal of universals,' a 'principle.' (P.R. 31)   You also use, by implication, the term 'form.' I judge you would not object to the term 'essence?'" Whitehead replied: "correct." "Yet, you speak of 'each event as an individual matter of fact issuing from an individualisation of the substrata activity (creativity).'" (S.M.W. 99.[14] See also P.R. 32).

Question--"Do you mean, more specifically, that the 'principle' or 'essence'--'creativity'--is exemplified in particular actual entities during their process of self-creative development. In this sense 'creativity' is a character which underlies all occasions." (S.M.W. 248)   Whitehead answered: "Yes."

Whitehead admitted that he applies the term "creativity" to both (a) the eternal object "creativity" and (b) the exemplifications of this eternal object. Most EOs are contingent potentialities--in the sense that they do not have to be actually exemplified by an AE. (They are present to God's P nature.) Ultimate principles like "creativity" are not contingent possibilities--i.e., they receive exemplification in all actual entities, at all times.

Whitehead stated that he should have included in the "Category of the Ultimate" a reference to the potentiality of contingency as closely allied to disjunctive diversity. (See P.R. 31)

Whitehead made the point that there are two basic forms of actual creativity (disregarding more complex processes, propositions, etc.) (1) With reference to eternal objects, there is the transformation from an essence (EO) into an exemplification. (2) Actual entities contribute to other actual entities by a "conformation" of character. There is also the sense of the "whereness" (from out thereness) which accompanies the prehending awareness (the taking in) of content by one AE from another.

As a "double check" on the preceding discussion, and in order to clear up possible and actual misunderstanding concerning Whitehead's use of basic terms, the following "statements and questions" were introduced:

(J) "Question A: When you speak of 'creatures of creativity'; 'God, a non-temporal accident of creativity'; 'God, the outcome of creativity,' (see P.R. 10-11, 31, 135, 248), am I correct in assuming that you do not refer to the emergence of God and other actual entities from one reality other than an actual entity, but to the fact that actual entities are the outcome of a creative process, i.e., the internal process of self-creation (of an actual entity)? In this sense, they are 'creatures of creativity?'

Question B: I presume that you would say that creativity as essence is exemplified in various actual entities, hence the use of the term 'accident.'?

Question C: When you say creativity is conditioned by its creatures, do you mean that creativity can only take place through the medium of the activity of actual entities (creatures)? (P.R. 33)

Question D: When you say that creativity is actual in virtue of its accidents do you mean that the essence creativity is exemplified in particular actual entities (accidents)?"

Whitehead answered question A: "Yes," and commented that God (AE) is necessary to the world of other AEs and they are necessary to him. God is one actual entity immersed in the process of his own self-creation and the process of self-creation of other AEs. God is brought to the same level (as far as actuality is concerned) as anything else in the universe. White-head denied the claim of Augustine and Aquinas, that the more important is therefore the more actual. There are two sides to actuality: (a) limitation to an historic moment, (b) everlastingness--accounted for by God's C nature.

Whitehead answered question B: "Not exactly," and remarked that he means by "accident," "decision" (i.e., an AE is the ultimate source of its decisions).

"God an accident" is an expression of the development of God's C nature (which never loses its character as specious present). It is wholly controlled by (a) a decision as to possibilities to be realized (accomplished by God's P nature); (b) a decision as to how God is going to receive data from the historical world.

At this point I asked: (J) "Wouldn't it be wiser to say God's subjective aim decides? There is a related question: Is God's P nature--that particular systematization of 'possibilities'--the only one he could have?"

Whitehead replied that he cannot settle the question. But what God has decided, is the realm of possibilities for the universe. What he decided is a free decision. It is a standard of perfection for the universe.

Whitehead expressed regret that he had to confine himself to such brief space in Religion in the Making. He wanted to write a much longer book. Dean Sperry[5] restrained him.

Whitehead answered question C: "Yes," and remarked that this deals with causality. He would stress, in the process, objective immortality; real potentiality; objectifications. The concrete characters of creatures are conditions (data to be used in) of creativity--hence, the notion of "real" potentiality.

Whitehead answered question D: "Yes," and suggested that 'creativity is actual in virtue of its accidents' should be changed--'actual' to 'actualized.'

Propositions

I introduced a discussion of propositions by saying: (J) "You state, 'A proposition is a new kind of entity' (P.R. 282) yet you also say--'A . . . proposition is the potentiality of an actual world including a definite set of actual entities in a nexus of reactions involving the hypothetical ingression of a definite set of eternal objects.' (P.R. 282)--My problem is that, in contrast with the first (which states that a proposition is a new kind of entity),--the second quotation seems to imply that a proposition is to be identified with actual entities and eternal objects."

In response Whitehead said that a proposition is an EO (or group of EOs) used as a "suggestion" about actualities. A proposition is an entity (EO) quae possibility not as actualized fact. The outstanding characteristic of a proposition is that it should be "interesting". Whitehead reported, with sad amusement, that he had been told about a scholar who had the misfortune to be confined to a mental hospital. The poor chap spent his days pacing back and forth muttering "It is more important that a proposition be interesting than that it be true" (A.I. 313).

Value

In reply to a request for information about his theory of value Whitehead stated that one source of value involves enjoyment of the past. There is a danger here, though, that the AE's experience, if confined to this, may shrivel up and be useless. When an AE has a vivid realization of its full character which is its own immediate self-creation, and its own function as one of the conditioning facts of the future, it has a sense of importance (which is a recognition of its immortality). It is aware of its value. Self valuation (of an AE) implies a reference to the "place of that AE in God's nature." It is a seeing of itself from God's point of view.

I then asked the specific question: "How do you determine degrees of value?"

Whitehead replied that there is no value feeling connected with awareness of pure EOs. The value of the abstract rises from its "possibility for" the realm of concrete actual entities.

Whitehead then referred to his discussion of degrees of value in <u>Adventures of Ideas</u>--(the section on "Civilization".) He remarked that for a feeling of perfection there is no adequate analysis. But it is a matter of dimly felt presence of EOs. It is the lure of God's nature imminent in us.

Whitehead remarked that he is essentially Greek-- in that he regards the difference between morality and aesthetics as not fundamental. Roughly speaking morality involves distant pleasures; aesthetic values have more immediate pleasures.

In passing, he mentioned a basic problem of morality. It presupposes freedom "at the moment" yet there must be determinism, otherwise there can be no responsibility. Moral rules (e.g., Ten Commandments) save us the difficulty of making a moral judgment too frequently. In many situations our habits make us do the right thing. We don't even think of the possi- bility of evil behavior, let alone have to face and fight it in order to achieve the right procedure. Emphasizing the restricted nature of moral codes, with a chuckle Whitehead referred to the Ten Commandments as: "How to get along in Arabia".

In the course of discussing the topics referred to above, a few other phases of Whitehead's philosophy were 'touched on'.

(J) "Question--By the extensive continuum do you mean:--(1) A nexus of actualities,--'real potentiality' (P.R. 123-4; 434); or (2) Is it a 'locus' which per- sists and provides an emplacement for all the occasions of experience (A.I. 241); or (3) Is it a sub-realm of potentialities (eternal objects) within God's pri- mordial nature. (Emmet)"

Whitehead replied that "extensive continuum (1) "is the dominant real potentiality of this present epoch. "Extensive continuum (2) "is the dominant metaphysical notion of objective immortality and the intercausation of the world. In his discussion of

the extensive continuum, he talks about two kinds of
"(1)". "(3)" is an extensive continuum only in the
sense that it is exemplified in a "(1)". "Receptacle"
expresses the abstract general notion that all AEs
must arise with reference to certain other AEs. This
is the principle of "whereness". Real potentiality
is an exemplification of this general principle.

In answer to a question about his use of the
term "quantum" (P.R. 434) Whitehead stated that a
quantum is "that much"--i.e., it can't be analyzed
further without losing something. Quantum also
implies a pattern of more or less--a continuity in
which is vaguely manifested a character. A quantum
is an AE in its immediacy manifesting a certain subjective form and subjective aim.

Society

One important aspect of Whitehead's theory of
societies of actual entities was introduced by my
remark: (J) "As I understand it, any quality, or
characteristic, manifested by an organism or society,
must be based on the experience of (be found in) a
component actual entity (entities) of that society or
organism. Thus no novel qualities emerge, applicable
to the organism or society as such, i.e., which are
not found in one component actual entity (or in each
of a series of actual entities.)"

In reply Whitehead admitted that he has no
"category" describing the fact that a society manifests patterns and qualities other than those found
in the component actual entities. He said he should
have introduced a Category of "Emergence of Novelty".
In the doctrine (category) of "transmutation" he tried
to approach it, but didn't succeed. Under the headings:
Extension; Proposition; Coordinate Division--it might
have been considered. It comes under the heading of
"Whereness". Whitehead pointed out that, though he
hasn't formulated a Category of "Emergence" (in the
sense indicated above), he had noted the fact of
"pattern of society"--the pattern being not an element
in any one component AE. There is (a) the sense of
"oneness" of the body (one's own) or (b) the felt
unity of a "perceived" person--(In contrast to Hume)--a
young man doesn't dance with a flux of sense and then
say--Here is a "dear girl". He is aware at once of the
person's bodily aspect as such (a unity).

53

These remarks led Whitehead on to the comment that the harboring of propositions (i.e., something new as a possibility) is the bases of "life" or "living". (a) A "dead" society is one in which there is little or no conceptual novelty. A "living" society maintains conceptual novelty. The society can be seen to be functioning teleologically. (b) "Life" is also used in the sense that any AE is living, since any AE has conceptual prehensions. Some novelty is thus introduced.

Consciousness

(J) "Question--why do you restrict 'consciousness' to the felt contrast and identities of feelings of lures? (P.R. 286) Why not recognize the common usage of consciousness as synonymous with awareness (in the sense of conceptual apprehension and sensuous awareness)?"

In reply Whitehead contended that the mere prehension of a fact (thing) is not consciousness. We have consciousness only when the fact is picked out-- as distinct, and characterized by some concept (EO). We never get an experience of mere brute fact--there is always a tinge of consciousness. Consciousness is the stabilizing element in memory and thought. E.g., This is blue and nothing else.

fact	concept	excluding concepts
	(EOs)	(EOs)

He mentioned N.K. Smith's A Commentary to Kant's Critique of Pure Reason XLII, as offering a similar position to his on consciousness, i.e., consciousness involves a judgment. In consciousness, we have a proposition which applies or doesn't apply to an object, i.e., we judge it does or doesn't apply. Kant's transcendental aesthetic interested Whitehead. In a sense, his Process and Reality is a transcendental aesthetic--how concepts are found in experience, not imposed on it.

A graduate course with Whitehead served, above all else, to illuminate and illustrate his profound conviction that "Philosophy is at once general and concrete, critical and appreciative of direct intuition. It is not--or, at least, should not be--a

ferocious debate between irritable professors. It
is a survey of possibilities and their comparison
with actualities. In philosophy, the fact, the
theory, the alternatives, and the ideals, are
weighed together. Its gifts are insight and fore-
sight, and a sense of the worth of life, in short,
that sense of importance which nerves all civilized
effort." (A.I. 125)

Notes

1. Emphasis and material in brackets are not in the text.

2. See Philosophical Review, Vol. XLIV, No. 272, March 1937, pp. 170-77.

3. Emphasis added.

4. Whitehead used the term "sensuous" in place of the more usual "sensory."

5. Emphasis added.

6. See for example, D.W. Hall, "Of What use are Whitehead's Eternal Objects?", Journal of Philosophy, xxvii (1930), pp. 29-44.

7. Whitehead had an extensive stock of stories on "religious" topics. After all his father was a clergyman--Canon of Canterbury Cathedral. With considerable glee Whitehead reported that the Archbishop of Canterbury used to invite candidates into his study and ask them to preach a sermon. One freshman got wound up, felt he was on a street corner and acted the part. He shook his fists under the Archbishop's nose and bellowed out: "When did you last read your Bible sir?"

In an autobiographical mood Whitehead reported that one of the recollections of earliest childhood experience also had to do with an Archbishop of Canterbury. The "great man" was visiting Whitehead, Senior. Little Alfred was permitted to have "tea" with this select group. He had prunes with his milk. Like many another small boy, it occurred to him that a prune pit would serve as an excellent projectile if propelled by a skillfully flipped spoon. He tested his hypothesis and scored a direct hit on the nose of His Grace, the Archbishop. Undoubtedly subsequent events served to impress the error of this performance on the "seat of his understanding."

8. In the early days of the "Simpson Affair" the British people were agitated by rumours of the royal infatuation. The New York Times made use of the British Coat of Arms to "cover the situation." This

heraldic device portrays a lion on one side of a shield and a unicorn on the other. The <u>Times</u> cartoon shows the unicorn leaning across the shield whispering in the lion's ear. The King of Beasts registers shock and amazement. Not knowing Whitehead's attitude to the British royal family, I somewhat diffidently described the cartoon. He reacted with keen amusement.

9. Here again of course, Whitehead was referring to Edward VIII, the Prime Minister of Great Britain, and the Archbishop of Canterbury. History has it that the latter two exerted decisive pressure in forcing the abdication of the King.

10. See photostatic reproduction in A.H. Johnson, <u>Whitehead's Theory of Reality</u>, p. 214.

11. See photostatic reproduction in A.H. Johnson, <u>Whitehead's Theory of Reality</u>, p. 218.

12. In other words, he is not concerned with metaphysics.

13. Relevant issues are also raised by D.C. Moxley in "The Conception of God in the Philosophy of Whitehead," <u>Aristotelian Society Proceedings</u>, N.S. XXIV, pp. 157-86.

14. Emphasis not in text.

15. Harvard Divinity School.

CHAPTER 3

CORRESPONDENCE WITH WHITEHEAD

The six letters from Alfred North Whitehead, here reproduced, are not, and were not intended to be, expositions of profound philosophical insights (with the exception of one brief passage). They are representative samples of his correspondence with a "graduate student" who wrote a dissertation on Whitehead's theory of reality. The latter letters clearly demonstrate the continuing, kindly, friendly, interest which Whitehead manifest with reference to students who no longer walked within the confines of the Yard at Harvard.

After each letter an explanatory comment has been added.

(1)

984 Memorial Drive
Appᵗ 504 Radnor Hall
Oct 30 /36

Dear Johnson

It will give my wife
the greatest pleasure if your
wife and you can come to an
informal party (morning dress)
~~there~~ on Tuesday next from
8 p.m. onwards. The main
purpose is to hear the election
results which will come over the
radio at intervals. But we
hope to combine this with
conversation –

Very Truly Yrs
Alfred North Whitehead

Comments on Letter One

It is reported that during the early years of Whitehead's presence at Harvard (in the middle 20's) an informal weekly "open house" was held on Sunday afternoons in the Whitehead apartment. In later years, because of the state of his health, graduate students were invited at infrequent intervals.

The letter dated October 30, 1936 involved one such event. Approximately twenty graduate students and their wives gathered in the spacious book lined study of the Whiteheads' Radnor Hall apartment. The election returns very quickly indicated that Roosevelt was thrashing Alf Landon. This was obviously in accordance with the hopes of both Professor and Mrs. Whitehead. The radio was silenced and conversation flourished in small groups as the Whiteheads moved about chatting with their guests. Incidentally it "turned out" that "morning dress" (see letter) meant: ordinary business suit. Indeed some guests wore the standard graduate student uniform namely slacks, and sportscoat with leather patches reinforcing the elbows.

My only other purely social experience in the Whitehead home occurred in late April of 1937, just before leaving Harvard. One Sunday evening my wife and I were invited to come in for conversation. On that occasion Professor and Mrs. T. North Whitehead were the only other persons present. However, shortly after our arrival Mr. Felix Frankfurter, then Professor at Harvard Law School "popped in" (as was his custom). After meeting the young graduate student and his wife he manoeuvred Whitehead into a distant corner and rather obviously enquired "Who are they"? Apparently he received a satisfactory answer. During the rest of the evening he regaled us with stories of his boisterous youth in central Europe, and subsequent activities. It was interesting to learn that once he was challenged to a duel by a ferociously efficient swordsman but managed to talk his way out of danger by changing the mind of his pugnacious adversary.

It was obvious that Whitehead received visits from many distinguished people. For example, he appeared in class one morning and apologized for not being very well prepared and remarked that he had spent the previous evening chatting with the President of the League of Nations.

61

Harvard University
Cambridge Mass
April 14 - 1937

Dear Johnson

We have discussed together the various salient points of your thesis. It has interested me to note your reactions to various salient topics of my philosophic thought, and your own expositions and criticisms of them. As you know, I have not seen the completed thesis in final form. But I hope that you will publish your work either as a short book, or as a series of two or three articles, in some philosophical journal either in England or America — for example, Mind or The Philosophical Review, to name two among others.

Sincerely Yours
Alfred North Whitehead

Comments on Letter Two

The very generous letter dated April 14, 1937, was given to me as I returned to the University of Toronto to take Ph.D. examinations. The statement by Whitehead "I have not seen the complete thesis in final form", requires explanation and clarification. Whitehead was here "proceeding on the assumption" that my Toronto professor G.S. Brett would require some changes in the manuscript which he (Whitehead) had examined. Whitehead, further, thought that he would not be informed concerning Brett's suggested changes. As a matter of fact Professor Brett did not request any changes at all. Thus actually the manuscript which Whitehead examined was (contrary to expectations) indeed my thesis in its final and complete form. In any case he was correct in stating that "we have discussed together the various salient points of your thesis".

This letter has been included, not as an ostentatious "ego-booster", but rather to support the claim that my interpretations of some of Whitehead's basic concepts and theories are accurate.

(3)
1737 Cambridge St.
Cambridge Mass.
Feb. 23 - 1941

Dear Johnson
            Thanks for your nice,
warm birthday letter - It
was thoroughly appreciated -
You are quite right - the
attitude towards philosophy
is the essential point, namely
important for the regulation
of emotion, purpose, and thought.
Differences of phraseology

arise from diverse experiences,
and are not to be construed as
mere refutations –

Again, thanks for your
letter

most sincerely yours
Alfred North Whitehead

Comments on Letter Three

Whitehead's letter dated **February 23, 1941** is worthy of careful consideration. Unfortunately a copy of my letter which stimulated his comments about philosophy is not available. However its contents are obvious from his reply. In any case, it is clear that Whitehead assigns to philosophy a highly practical function, namely that of regulating emotion, purpose and thought. The emphasis is frequently ignored by those who are over-impressed by Whitehead's attempt to formulate a metaphysical system and his concern for categories. Further, it is well to note his comments on the relation of words and experience, and their status.

1737 Cambridge St.
Cambridge – Mass.
Sept 10 – 1943

Dear Johnson
It was very pleasant to hear from you – Of course give me as a reference, if it is of any use to you. Congratulations to your wife and yourself on your two young daughters – Children add a charm to life beyond anything else –

Yours ever
Alfred North Whitehead

Comments on Letter Four

Whitehead's continuing warm interest in the academic careers and the "fortunes of life" of former students is clearly illustrated in his letter dated September 10, 1943.

MRS. A. N. WHITEHEAD
1737 CAMBRIDGE STREET
CAMBRIDGE 38, MASSACHUSETTS, U. S. A.

Wednesday, Feb. 21 1945

Dear Prof: Johnson
　　　　Thank you very warmly
for your kind birthday greetings
Such letters are very stimulating to
old people -
By accident I was reading your article
on me in the Journal of 'Philos. etc' -
It was stimulating to feel that some of
you have got something from my writings.
Of course they lack much that ought to
be there - Anyhow you pleased me
much.
　　　　　Yours ever
　　Alfred North Whitehead

Comments on Letter Five

　　Alfred North Whitehead was born February 15, 1861.
A number of his students were in the habit of sending
him birthday greetings each year.

　　The article to which he referred in his letter of
February 21, 1945 is, as far as I can determine (in the
absence of exact identification by him); "Truth, Beauty
and Goodness in the philosophy of A.N. Whitehead",
Philosophy of Science, Vol. 11, No. 1, January 1944.)

(6)

A. N. WHITEHEAD
1737 CAMBRIDGE STREET
CAMBRIDGE 38, MASSACHUSETTS, U. S. A.

Saturday - Dec. 14. 1946

Dear Prof: Johnson

I have no objection to your proposed reprint of your article in bookform. namely your article = Philos. of Science - July 1946.

Sincerely yrs
Alfred North Whitehead

Comments on Letter Six

The title of the article to which Whitehead refers is "The Wit and Wisdom of Whitehead" (published in Philosophy of Science Vol. 13, No. 3, 1946).

Shortly after the publication of this article I received a letter from Mr. Melvin L. Arnold, director of the Beacon Press, Boston, Mass. stating that he would like to republish the article in book form. I expressed interest and suggested that an introductory essay be included, namely my "Alfred North Whitehead", which had appeared in the University of Toronto Quarterly, Vol. 15, No. 4, July 1946. This was agreed and The Wit and Wisdom of Whitehead appeared in 1947.

CHAPTER 4

PAUL WEISS AND OTHERS ON:

WHITEHEAD AS TEACHER

I

The "pictures" of Whitehead in the classroom and conducting individualized tutorials, as presented in Chapters 1 and 2 of this volume, differ markedly, at some crucial points, from those provided by Paul Weiss in his "Recollections of Alfred North Whitehead."[1]

It should be realized that his discussion is, for the most part, dated "as of 1927-29". Mine applies to Whitehead's "performance" in 1936-37. The lack of humor, fumbling for answers, the general inadequacy of Whitehead as teacher (reported by Weiss, pp. 44,47) did not characterize the Whitehead I met in 1936-37. Indeed the exact opposite was the case.

I have already commented on his apparent lack of organization (more apparent than real). It is true that Whitehead did not encourage discussion during a "class hour"--but he was "willing and able" afterwards. His answers were usually clear and crisp (when the subject matter permitted it). His humorous stories and brilliant "turns of phrase" were not only informative but also stimulating and refreshing. Chapter 1 and 2 of this volume provide detailed support for what I have just reported, and further heighten the contrast between my 1936-37 picture of Whitehead as classroom lecturer and Weiss' earlier version.

Like Weiss, I found that Whitehead did not know the names of most members of his classes--a few graduate students being an exception. In this defect Whitehead was not unique. Notwithstanding this, he established effective rapport with most class members. He was also impressive in "handling" visitors. When some members of the Yale football team appeared and requested permission to attend a lecture--he was most gracious, and chatted with them at length, when the lecture was over.

69

In all fairness to Weiss, it must be emphasized
that after portraying Whitehead's lecture style as
involving many defects (noted above), he reported
that, on many occasions, after considerable hesitation, Whitehead would make brilliant and thought-
provoking comments which graduate student Paul Weiss
valued highly (p. 44, 47) even if undergraduates did
not derive as much benefit therefrom. In 1936-37,
I found little of the negative characteristics and
many instances of the positive.

In brief, at this later date, I do not think
that some faculty members and some students regarded
Whitehead as a somewhat Pickwickian person--concerning
whose performance as a teacher one could legitimately
protest (pp. 44-45)--whatever was the case in 1927-29.

In addition to specific reports on Whitehead
as teacher, Weiss referred to some more general
personality traits which Whitehead manifested in the
teaching context and in the wider 'world' of human
relations of all sorts.

Weiss stated that in dealing with people,
Whitehead never criticized a person directly. He
"always had kind things to say" (p. 45). Weiss then
remarked that in such circumstances persons thought
that they were being praised, whereas, as a matter of
fact, Whitehead was merely being polite! It is indeed
the case that Whitehead, both in writing and speaking,
was sometimes overgenerous in his references to the
work of other men. This has led to mistaken notions
of detailed "kinships" between, for example, Whitehead
and Spinoza, Whitehead and Bradley--at all points, not
just a few very general ones. I recall noting an
advertisement, in The Journal of Philosophy, for a re-
issue of the writings of G.H. Mead. Included were
some very complimentary remarks by A.N. Whitehead.
When I mentioned this to him he chuckled and said (in
effect): Oh well, you have to say something pleasant
in such cases. However, there was "another side",
or sort, of reaction, in Whitehead's relation with his
fellow-men. I have never forgotten being ushered into
his study (by the maid) just as he was finishing a
session with another student. The poor chap had
apparently been "slacking" in his assignments. Though
it was near the beginning of the fall term, Whitehead
in unmistakably firm tones, informed the student that

perhaps he could return for another session in the spring. In brief, cool firmness, not soft "niceness" characterized Whitehead in this case. Further, one should recall Whitehead's strong negative reactions to the theory and practices of some professional educators: The Aims of Education (Chapter 1) provides plenty of examples of a Whitehead who was "not nice" to his fellow men. For instance, he accused some of his colleagues of "soul murder", or referred to them as "Whitehead sepulchers".

Indeed Weiss gives evidence of the two aspects of Whitehead's character (p. 53). He reports that Whitehead was very unwilling to accept criticism of his Process and Reality. Whitehead reacted in a strong negative fashion (and Mrs. Whitehead even more so!) (p. 46).

In this context Weiss made the point that, in his opinion, Whitehead had a kind of public naivety but there was also "a very strong, tough, steel-like interior" (p. 53) which led Whitehead to react vigorously.

My own experience in criticizing Whitehead rather intensely is general, and Process and Reality in particular--was not of this sort. Whitehead took no umbrage. Indeed, he admitted serious defects with cheerful candor. His marginal notes on my Ph.D. thesis are an illustration of this type of reaction (see my Whitehead's Theory of Reality, Appendix B). Further (to reiterate), contrary to Weiss' reports (p. 44), when confronted by criticism he did not mutter, "Uh, uh" and stare at the wall or blackboard and utter limp acquiescence. Usually he answered quickly and clearly in accordance with the relevant tenets of his philosophical system (if the question permitted such an answer), and dealt effectively with criticisms. (See for example Chapter 2 of this volume.)

More specifically, my experience was very different from that of Weiss. He prepared a series of questions which he submitted to Whitehead. No direct, or satisfactory, answers were received (p. 48). My experience, reported in Chapter 2 of this book, was the exact opposite. To each question I raised, a direct and coherent answer was forthcoming, in some cases at considerable length. There was no attempt at diversion, or slipping off into some other area of discussion (p. 48).

Also, unlike Weiss (p. 53) I found Whitehead very willing to discuss (minute details of) Process and Reality.

I was surprised to find Weiss stating, with reference to Whitehead's negative reaction to his criticism of Process and Reality--that Whitehead was "a Victorian" in his attitude towards the young, women, blacks, Indians--quite "conservative" (p. 46). On the contrary, Whitehead struck me as being a "Renaissance" type of man, trying to live up to his stress on "adventure" as one of the main aspects of civilized life. I recall his remark that "the pure conservative is fighting against the essence of the Universe" (A.I. 354). Indeed, Whitehead's approach to the Universe exemplified the Renaissance open-mindedness: "nothing common or unclear".

His concern for Women's rights has recently been documented.[2] As noted earlier, Whitehead was quite prepared to take seriously the criticisms of his work offered by at least one young person. I have reason to believe that there were others. I have no direct evidence to submit concerning his attitude to "blacks and Indians", but I am reminded of his criticisms of slavery in Adventures of Ideas (pp. 14, 15, 28).

Incidentally, I agree with Weiss when he suggests that Whitehead would be amazed by the fact that Process and Reality is regarded as the book to be read in order to understand Whitehead--the rest can be safely neglected. (p. 47)

Weiss aptly notes that Whitehead was extremely tentative in some of his pronouncements (he offered only a "likely story" p. 55)--hence his willingness to accept criticism, at least on occasion. He laughed appreciatively at Paul Weiss' criticism of his theory of types in Principia Mathematica. Whitehead regarded many of his (own) ideas as "opening up", adventures, searches for expression of insights into, the nature of things (p. 47). However, it does not seem accurate, to me, to claim that Whitehead had no firm doctrines (p. 55)--or, as Weiss puts it: He was "always changing his mind. I don't think that there was a definite doctrine that he was maintaining". (p. 48)

In reaction to this claim, one is likely to retort: Surely the categoreal scheme outlined in Process and Reality pp. 27-42 was something to which he adhered from its formulation to the end of his career. It must be born in mind that he did also use an alternate non-technical categoreal scheme (see Section III of this book). All categories were (are) expressions of a few basic insights which Whitehead always took seriously. On the basis of other such insights he based other less general doctrines (than those expressed in the Process and Reality, pp. 27-42, Categoreal schemes). One recalls his adherence to the theory that "peace" is a basic ingredient in genuinely civilized life. He adhered without digression to many religious, political, educational and other doctrines (see A.H. Johnson, Whitehead's Philosophy of Civilization).

Weiss' portrait of Whitehead as thesis supervisor (p. 48) does not do justice to the man I knew. I raised a series of questions which Whitehead discussed clearly and in detail. I then wrote my thesis and left it with him for perusal and comment. He commented at length and made some marginal notes. In general, when I interpreted him correctly he said so. When I misinterpreted him, he left no doubt in my mind that such was the case--and helped me try to oversome such defects.

How can one explain the crucial differences in the two pictures of Whitehead? Perhaps it is a case of: With the passage of time Whitehead succeeded in acquiring many skills suitable for a North American style classroom performance. Likewise, he developed greater "tutorial" facility. That he did not acquire all the "tricks of the trade" is not strange in view of his age and the various activities in which he was engaged.

The fact remains: the "Paul Weiss" description of "Whitehead as Teacher" is strikingly different from the A.H. Johnson "version".

II

At this point it is relevant to remind ourselves that Whitehead's former student, colleague and "sometime" friend--Bertrand Russell, provides a very diverse "portrait" of Whitehead the man. On the one hand he appears as a brilliant and thorough scholar, a devoted and highly effective teacher, a warm friend, a charming social being. On the other hand, Whitehead is presented as an insensitive husband, a man in danger of slipping into insanity, a person given to private mutterings about his own shortcomings, a bumbling incompetent in personal financial matters. Further, he didn't answer letters! This, according to Russell, was Alfred North Whitehead in his early years of the twentieth century.[3]

The Alfred North Whitehead of 1936-37 had all of the excellences and none of the defects listed by Russell--as far as one graduate student was concerned. This judgment was based on an academic year of weekly private tutorials an hour long with intense discussion, regular attendance three times a week at lectures, two lengthy social occasions in the Whitehead home, and a long slow walk from "The Yard" to Radnor Hall on the Charles River where Whitehead's apartment was located. At least one former student experienced absolutely no difficulty, subsequently, in receiving prompt replies to letters written to Whitehead.[4] It is true that on retirement he moved to an apartment less grand than the one in Radnor Hall. However, that sort of thing frequently happens when a professor retires.

The ready humor, the evident full enjoyment of life, the obvious intellectual and social competence which characterized Whitehead in 1936-37--none of these apparently "forced"--all this does not indicate the presence of a "sick soul". Indeed, all graduate students who knew Whitehead at all well, shared my very favorable reaction.

III

It is significant that Joseph G. Brennan, who attended Whitehead's lectures on Cosmologies in the fall of 1934, presents a picture of Whitehead as teacher very similar to mine.[5]

Like Brennan I was impressed by Whitehead's energy, good humor and relatively informal manner of lecturing. The reference to his style as that of an "amiable chat" is very apt.

In Brennan's account there are traces of the apparent "unease" mentioned by Weiss. He reports that Whitehead often paused "to gaze out the nearest window" (p. 515). In 1936-37 this tendency was reduced to a very scanty minimum. In any case, staring out a window may indicate concentration rather than maladjustment to the classroom situation.

Brennan's picture of Whitehead humorously heaping ridicule on himself because of his inability to find a piece of chalk, is not the behavior of a man ill-at-ease before students. His "funny stories" about colleagues at Trinity College Cambridge are not indicative of a man lacking in control of himself or the situation confronting him.

When told by Brennan that he had studied with the Jesuits of Boston College, Whitehead reacted with a feigned horror at the poor impression his lack of clarity would make on Brennan. This was typical of Whitehead's ease in social relations with his students (p. 516).

Worthy of note is Brennan's remark in 1978 that "looking back now, I find it hard to describe the atmosphere of reverent awe that surrounded the philosopher in those days" (p. 516). Very obviously, even if the account is somewhat exaggerated, there is no suggestion of the bumbling inefficiency and incompetence with which some faculty and students charged Whitehead in 1927-29--according to Weiss. In brief, as Brennan put it: "Whitehead's classroom lectures were entirely enjoyable" (p. 517). In like fashion the young ladies of Radcliffe, who listened to his lectures on Cosmology in 1931-32, described him as "so dear" (p. 517).

Among the "revealing" stories about Whitehead (not otherwise readily available) is Brennan's description of Whitehead's encounter with two Radcliffe girls and a shoe shine man in Harvard Square. The "boot black" was anxious to add further shine to the philosopher's shoes. On the other hand, he was more anxious to discuss their Columbus Day holiday plans with the young ladies of Radcliffe. Here again Whitehead's efficiency as a social being was clearly manifest.

75

There is also evidence in Brennan's essay to support the contention that Whitehead was not always "mild and nice" in dealing with students and staff. There is an example, via Bertrand Russell, of a case where Whitehead showed a wily sharpness and shrewdness in "getting his way" in committees (p. 517). In Brennan's account of Whitehead's lectures on Cosmologies there are reproduced some of the very effectual illustrations which were employed, for example: his squirrel story, to stress the importance of mathematics; or the skillful use of quotations from Cohen's Reason and Nature and Russell's Freedom and Organization to demonstrate the defects of narrow positivism.

The general evaluation which Brennan assigned to Whitehead as teacher is that he was a dynamic, witty, able practitioner of the art of teaching and, in general, an effective human being of great personal charm in social relations. Thus, to repeat, there is considerable support in Brennan's essay for my picture of Whitehead as he was in 1937--in contrast, in some major respects, to what Weiss says about him as of 1927-29. It is only fair to note here that Weiss does, on occasion, refer to Whitehead's social charm and his ability to establish rapport with some of his students.

It should be stressed that Brennan's essay provides a useful indication of the content of Whitehead's Cosmologies course. Unlike my reference to it, in Chapter 1 of this volume, he does not attempt a reconstruction of typical lectures. Rather he tries to list and illustrate the sort of topics Whitehead discussed in the course. This provides somewhat more detailed information, at some points, than my technique of listing the required reading in the course to supplement representative samples of lectures.

It is well to observe that there are a few errors in an otherwise very useful essay. He wrongly reports the date of Whitehead's death as 1948. Actually it occurred December 30, 1947. A more serious error, concerning the content of Whitehead's philosophy, is the statement that "God is the entity ultimately responsible for Reality being as it is and not otherwise" (p. 518).

As a matter of fact, for Whitehead, the primordial nature of God organizes the realm of eternal objects and makes them available for possible use by newly arising actual entities (actual entities are the final <u>real</u> things of which the world is made). But what the realm of actual entities is, depends ultimately on choices made by individual actual entities--making use of data provided by other actual entities--including God (see A.H. Johnson, <u>Whitehead's Theory of Reality</u>, pp. 39-41). This being so, it is obvious that Brennan is again erroneous when he states that 'God is the cosmological factor that elicits actuality from possibility" (p. 524). He is also wrong in claiming that there are only <u>two</u> sides to Whitehead's God. As a matter of fact there are three: (1) Primordial, (2) Consequent, (3) Superject (see <u>P.R.</u> 532).

Finally, by way of comment--certainly not put forward as a serious criticism--I wish to take issue with Brennan's several references to the "clerical appearance" of Whitehead. For example, he states: "He seemed like a benevolent vicar from a nineteenth century English novel" (p. 515). Speaking as a person who was brought up in the home of a clergyman (my grandfather's) and having had a good deal to do with 'gentlemen of the cloth" in the early part of my life, and having read many 19th century English novels, I must say that Whitehead did not strike me as having a clerical appearance or characteristics.

IV

In "The Reader Replies" section of <u>The American Scholar</u>, Vol. 48, No. 4, Autumn 1979, pp. 573-76), Philip H. Rhinelander outlines two major criticisms of Brennan's article. It turns out to be chiefly criticisms of Brennan's approach to his topic. However, the "reply" does have a bearing on "the matter before us".

Like other commentators on Whitehead's performance, he remarks that "the teacher" was usually better" when on a "one to one" relation with his students than when confronted by a large class. Whitehead's kindly tolerance of student deficiencies, his generous praise of student effort, his willingness to accept criticism, are also noted very appropriately.

Rhinelander points out that a full discussion of Whitehead as teacher should involve reference to his exposition of the theory of good teaching as outlined in The Aims of Education and elsewhere. (Rhinelander's first criticism of Brennan is that he makes no reference to this theoretical background). He then proceeds to state: "That his [Whitehead's] lectures were often disorganized and usually obscure is certainly true, as Professor Brennan rightly notes" (p. 574). As a matter of fact, as has been demonstrated in my reconstruction of typical Whitehead lectures (in Chapter 1 of this volume)--these evaluations are not correct. (Incidentally Brennan does not make these criticisms!)

Rhinelander's second criticism of Brennan is concerned with the purpose of a course of Cosmology. It raises some interesting issues as to the meaning of the term: "Cosmology". It is made clear that Rhinelander disagrees with Brennan.

V

During the academic year 1926-27, George Bosworth Burch attended Whitehead's lecture course: "Philosophy of Science: General Metaphysical Problems". His notes, edited by Dwight C. Stewart, were published in Process Studies, Vol. 4, No.3, Fall 1974, pp. 199-206.

In view of the fact that Paul Weiss came to Harvard as a graduate student in February 1927, and refers (in his "Recollections") to Burch's questions in the class which both attended, it is very relevant to compare (if possible) Weiss' description of Whitehead as teacher with Burch's presentation. Unfortunately difficulties confront us. The nature and extent of the "editing" of Burch's notes by Stewart is not indicated. Further, it is not clear to what degree (if any) Burch edited (i.e., reorganized or omitted) Whitehead's remarks. Further, Burch does not provide any direct evaluation of Whitehead's skill (or otherwise) as a teacher. Finally, Stewart organized Burch's notes under various headings. Obviously each section contains notes on more than one lecture. For example, the section entitled "Lectures by Professor Whitehead" was identified by Burch as notes on lectures delivered February 26 and March 1 1927.

Given all these difficulties, one can not place too much weight on the organization (or lack of it)--varying degrees of order found in the various sections. The content of the section entitled "Lectures by Professor Whitehead on Metaphysics" is likely to be considered as quite coherent by most readers. Such is not the case concerning "Lectures by Professor Whitehead on Descartes".

Be that as it may, one fact is worthy of very careful note. At this time Weiss indicates that Whitehead, while capable of brilliant and stimulating "turns of phrase"--aphorisms--did not inject humor into his lectures.

In the section entitled "Lectures by Professor Whitehead: Introduction: (p. 201) it is recorded that Burch heard examples of Whiteheadian aphorisms which were characterized by a subtle and urbane humor--which Weiss seems to have missed. The edited notes include the following: "We must not ignore the inexplicable, we should imitate our ancestors who beat gongs when the moon was eclipsed". Consider also: "The old rationalism was founded on the ideal of the clear intellect--but there is no such intellect. Some facts are luminously obvious, but the rest of our experience is obscured in a deep penumbrial shadow with reference to which our intellectual faculty varies from that of a savage to that of a jelly-fish." The same sophisticated humor is evident in the remark that "Scientists who are clear in their concepts are at least thirty years behind their times."

VI

Another "late 20's" graduate student at Harvard who observed Whitehead in action was F. Hilton Page. He arrived in the fall of 1928. His reactions (initial and subsequent) to Whitehead (as teacher) are set out in "A.N. Whitehead: A Pupil's Tribute" (The Dalhousie Review, April 1948).

79

Page provides an excellent report on Whitehead's physical characteristics, including his air of "extreme neatness and cleanliness". He then stresses his impression of gracious, kindly, generous goodness. Indeed Page was more impressed, at first meeting, by the professor's moral, rather than by his intellectual, greatness. In his article, Page develops at considerable length the point stressed by Brennan: Whitehead's Victorian clerical appearance. He also uses the descriptive term: Venerable.

As Whitehead's course of lectures proceeded, Page was increasingly struck by the apparent contrast between the technical difficulties of the content (manifesting great intellectual power) and the manner of presentation: unpretentious, "occasionally almost child-like simplicity". But there could be no doubt of the engaging, persuasive, skill in discussing ideas which undoubtedly were very "difficult" for most members of the audience. Page reports that Whitehead's cheerful, humorous, excited and enthusiastic approach to philosophical issues was almost inescapably contageous in many instances.

It is important to note that Page's very favorable description of Whitehead as teacher is tempered by reference to the aspect which Weiss stresses (to a greater extent than Page), namely Whitehead's difficulty "sometimes" (at this period) in expressing himself effectively in the classroom.

On balance, and predominantly, in Page's opinion, Whitehead had the characteristics of a great teacher. He conveyed a sense of the importance of his subject, and aroused the student's agreement and the desire to continue his own investigations in that field of knowledge.

Whitehead's generosity, and indeed gentleness, in dealing with struggling serious students, is stressed by Page, but here again his account is aptly balanced by the remark that Whitehead could be (and was), on occasion, drastic in condemning superficial (so-called "literary") approaches to important issues.

In brief, as in the case of Brennan's description, there is considerable contrast at least as to emphasis (and some content) with Weiss's "late 20's" picture of Whitehead as teacher. Ultimately one can only strive to be as accurate as possible--welcome agreement-- wonder at (and about) disagreement.

Notes

1. *Process Studies*, Vol. 10, Nos. 1-2, Spring-Summer 1980, pp. 44-56. All page references to Weiss will be to this article. This is an interview by L.W. Ford.)

2. *Process Studies*, Vol. 7, No. 1, pp. 37-39.

3. See *Autobiography of Bertrand Russell 1872-1914*, Allen and Unwin, London, 1967, pp. 127-30; Ronald W. Clark, *The Life of Bertrand Russell*, Jonathon Cape and Weiderfeld and Nicolson, London, 1975, pp. 87-117.

4. See Chapter 3 of this volume.

5. Joseph G. Brennan, "Alfred North Whitehead Plato's Lost Dialogue", *The American Scholar*, Vol. 47, No.4, 1978, pp. 515-24. All references to Brennan will be to this article.

SECTION   TWO

DIFFICULTIES WITH SPECIFIC TECHNICAL CONCEPTS

CHAPTER 5

HARTSHORNE'S INTERPRETATION OF WHITEHEAD

I

One of Charles Hartshorne's most strongly held, and influential, views is that Whitehead should be interpreted as contending that: all past actual entities are retained in God (more specifically, God's consequent nature) in their individual entirety, i.e., living vividness and immediacy, individual identity and completeness of unity.[1] Hartshorne admits that there are passages in Whitehead's writings which seem to cast doubt on this interpretation, but he is convinced that his conclusion is sound.

On the basis of (a) an extensive examination of the relevant passages, (b) a careful discussion of the topic with Whitehead, and (c) Whitehead's written comments (and absence of objections) on the margins of a thesis in which I took issue with the view held by Hartshorne--it is here contended that Hartshorne's interpretation of Whitehead, at this point, is mistaken.

It is essential to understand fully what Whitehead means when he states that "the 'consequent nature' of God is the physical prehension by God of the actualities of the evolving universe" (P.R. 134) --or to stress another aspect: the consequent nature of God is "the objectification of the world in God" (P.R. 523). In discussing the process by which an ordinary actual entity (i.e., one other than God) becomes involved in prehension by God, and objectification in God--Whitehead stresses the point that these results can only occur after the prehended and objectified actual entity, as such, has gone out of existence. In brief, what occurs is an appropriation of the dead by the living. Specifically, Whitehead states: "Actuality in perishing acquires objectivity, while it loses subjective immediacy." (P.R. 44);--Its "own internal existence has evaporated, worn out and satisfied" (P.R. 336). (See also this book, pp. 35, 47.)

In view of such statements it is difficult to understand, and/or accept, Hartshorne's remark that to become past, or to perish, is not to alter.[2]

85

Further statements by Whitehead compound the difficulties attendant on Hartshorne's interpretation of Whitehead's theory of the relation of actual entities to the consequent nature of God. For example, consider this: "Each actuality in the temporal world has its reception into God's nature. The corresponding element in God's nature is not temporal actuality, but is the transmutation of that temporal actuality" (P.R. 531). In a similar vein, one finds Whitehead stating that: "Each novel actuality in the temporal world contributes such elements as it can to realization in God" (P.R. 134). The contrast between temporal actualities and the corresponding, or contributing, elements in God's experience is striking. It is surely clear that the temporal actualities are not, as such, present in God--rather, only some elements are there, "corresponding" to (though not identical with) the temporal actuality.

In one of the preceding passages, Whitehead claimed that in God's nature there is transmutation of elements from the temporal world. Likewise he refers to the realization of the temporal world by its (elements of its) inclusion in God's nature and transformation by his wisdom.(P.R. 524) It is well to consider carefully what Whitehead means by "realization" in this context. It seems to imply: use by God in accordance with His wisdom, resulting in a change, i.e., transformation.

The factor of altering of the temporal world of actual entities by God's prehension, and hence their objectification in him--is expressed by Whitehead in many different terms. In addition to those already noted, he refers to the fluent world of actuality being everlasting in God. He also speaks of the temporal world being "perfected", and of its reformation, due to its reception in God.(P.R. 527) He follows this by stating that "the temporal occasions are completed by their everlasting union with their transformed selves, purged into conformation with the eternal order" (P.R. 527).

Despite all these statements Hartshorne, and others who share his interpretation, find comfort and apparent support in a series of apparently conflicting, indeed opposing, pronouncements by Whitehead. Consider, for example, the remark that God's consequent nature

has "the property of combining creative advance with
the retention of mutual immediacy" (P.R. 524-25).
There is also a reference to "the perfected actuality
[God] in which the many are one everlastingly without
the qualification of any loss of individual identity
or of completeness of unity" (P.R. 532). However, it
is more than plausible to claim (contrary to Hartshorne) that these references to "immediacy", "individuality", "identity", and "unity"--are not directed
to the inner life of ordinary actual entities, reputed
by Hartshorne to be retained unchanged in God. Rather,
Whitehead is discussing elements of God's inner life.
These elements are derived from ordinary actual entities,
but are not actual entities as such.

When in conversation with Whitehead, I proposed
this anti-Hartshorne interpretation of his (Whitehead's)
reference to "immediacy", quoted above, he accepted it.[3]
Also, he did not object when I used this (my) interpretation in the thesis which I wrote under his supervision.

Yet an apparently serious "stumbling block" remains.
Consider the often quoted Whitehead remark that in God's
experience of the world of ordinary temporal actual
entities, "there is no loss, no obstruction" (P.R. 524).
Nevertheless, on the next page this sweeping generalization is drastically qualified: "loses nothing that can
be saved" (P.R. 525).

It is interesting to note that this important comment is set in the context of a discussion of the relation to God of emotionally charged activities and
reactions occurring in the temporal world. Here, and
also elsewhere, he is dealing not with actual entities
but with emotional states such as joy, sorrow, suffering,
and characteristics of reactions, e.g., failure and
triumph. Yet, in this context, the familiar references
to immediacy, novelty, a perfected system are repeated.

Particularly worthy of note is the obvious implication of elimination and revision carried out by
inclusion in God's nature. God prehends "every actuality for what it can be in such a perfected system"
(P.R. 525). Relevant here also is the following remark,
"the immediacy of sorrow and pain is transformed into
an element of triumph" (P.R. 531). Yet, the "talk" of
one and many, novelty and endurance, in the context of
emotional illustrations, involves a troublesome statement that God's consequent nature results in "the

perfect multiplicity of the attainment" . . . "of self-existence" (P.R. 530). In an outburst of lyrical prose, Whitehead suggests the true self-attainment, namely a concern for value beyond oneself, is, in a very real sense, inclusion in a perfected system.

It must be emphasized that in the process of expounding, and interpreting, his views, Whitehead sometimes makes statements that are not entirely accurate expressions of his actual point of view. He later corrects them or admits that they require correction. For example, in writing my thesis, attention was called to a number of instances of Whitehead's inaccuracy and apparent carelessness. In some cases he was quite prepared to admit the validity of these criticisms. This is evident from the marginal notes he appended to a number of pages of the thesis.[4] Of particular significance, to the present discussion, is Whitehead's statement that "the consequent nature of God is composed of a multiplicity of elements with individual self-realization" (P.R. 531). When I objected to this on the grounds that it was not a satisfactory exposition of Whitehead's real meaning, he accepted this criticism. (W.T.R. 216)

Specifically, aspects of the statement are open to criticism because of inaccuracy or inadequacy of expression. (a) It is said in the context of the (following) statement that God's consequent nature "is just as much a multiplicity as it is a unity" (P.R. 531). It is of course true that for Whitehead God's consequent nature is composed of a number of (multiplicity of) prehensions. In this sense, it is composed of a multiplicity of elements. But the far more crucial point is that God's consequent nature is a unity of these many prehensions--not just the bare togetherness of many elements without unifying aim or purpose. (b) The reference to "elements with individual self-realization" is misleading in view of Whitehead's usual claim that actual entities are self-created--in the sense of self-realizing. On the other hand, the elements of the consequent nature of God are not actual entities.

Further support for my interpretation of the relation of ordinary actual entities and God is found in a marginal note on my thesis (see W.T.R. 217). Here very clearly Whitehead accepts the interpretation that some of the available data are not prehended by God.

Indeed in a footnote Whitehead refers to negative prehension, i.e., elimination, as having a place in God's experience.

As noted earlier, Chapter 2 of this book is a report of a year-long series of private tutorial sessions with Whitehead during the academic year 1936-37. Numerous items appear which have an important bearing on the topic of this chapter. The following passage is of particular significance: "I said (J): I judge that when you refer to God retaining immediacy (P.R. 530) the immediacy God retains is his own, not that of actual entities objectified in him. Some phases of their being are eliminated as they pass into God. When you say nothing is lost, don't you mean that in God as consequent, actual entities are transformed? Nothing is lost which can be saved (i.e., is worthy of being saved)." In reply, Whitehead commented that God's immediacy doesn't die. There is no elimination in God's nature as such. There is, of course, elimination of some of the data presented for inclusion in God's nature.

It is extremely interesting to observe Charles Hartshorne's reaction to my report of these tutorial sessions with Whitehead, in particular, to the topics under discussion in this chapter. Hartshorne saw most of my report when he read the manuscript of my "Whitehead As Teacher and Philosopher" before it appeared in Philosophy and Phenomenological Research, Volume 29, No.3, 1969. In a letter to me, undated but designated as referring to "Whitehead as Teacher" article (see p. 99 of this volume), Hartshorne stated: "You seem to prove me wrong in taking [by your showing] Whitehead to assert omission or negative prehension even in God's prehension. I retain my view that this is a mistake on his part, but it does seem deliberate."

In other words, Hartshorne here is apparently prepared (but with considerable hesitation) to admit that Whitehead's theory of the consequent nature of God involves some loss, i.e., not everything is saved from the world of antecedent actual entities. The point that, in Whitehead's theory, God engages in negative prehensions, is designated by Hartshorne, in a subsequent passage, as "a decisive clarification". After dealing with another topic, Hartshorne (in this letter) returns to the "negative prehension by God" theme. There he remarks: "I am . . . still not certain that

Whitehead always thought the same, e.g., whether or not God omits aspects. But I certainly see my interpretation of his meaning as made considerably less probably [probable?] by your testimony."

Obviously, as he wrote the letter, Hartshorne shifted from an "acceptance with hesitation" approach to negative prehension by God (in Whitehead's theory)-- to the admission that his (Hartshorne's) interpretation (Whitehead does not attribute negative prehension to God) is rendered considerably less plausible-- by my report of tutorial sessions with Whitehead. It is only fair to emphasize that this letter should not be taken to be Hartshorne's final word on the subject!

Incidentally, it is worthy of note that in a letter dated September 7, 1945 (see p. 96 of this volume) Hartshorne indicates his willingness to admit that he was wrong in assigning to Whitehead the theory that in God's consequent nature all contents of entities are retained without loss. Sadly, Hartshorne claims that Whitehead should have held a view which Hartshorne mistakenly attributed to him.

Notes

1. See for example: "The Immortality of the Past," The Review of Metaphysics, Vol. 7, pp. 98-112; "Whitehead's Idea of God", The Philosophy of Alfred North Whitehead, (P.A. Schilpp, ed.) pp. 519, 529, 538.

2. "The Immortality of Past", p. 109.

3. See Chapter 2 of this volume, pp. 42-43.

4. See photostatic reproductions on pages 214, 216, 218, 219, 220, 222 of my Whitehead's Theory of Reality, Dover Publications, New York, 1962.

Correspondence with Charles Hartshorne--Comments

No one has done more to arouse and "keep fresh" interest in the philosophy of Alfred North Whitehead than Charles Hartshorne (with the exception of Whitehead himself).

When I first met Professor Hartshorne, at the University of Chicago in 1934, I was particularly impressed by his enthusiasm and generosity of spirit, his willingness to assist students, of whatever status, in their attempts to understand Whitehead's philosophy. I have profited greatly from my first and subsequent association with Charles Hartshorne. However, early in this association I found it necessary to disagree with some of his interpretations of Whitehead, at several crucial points--in particular his interpretation of Whitehead's theory of the consequent nature of God.

The two letters referred to previously are not the only items of correspondence with Hartshorne. Over the years from 1938 on to the present, I have had the benefit of considerable written communication with him concerning some of my published material and other matters of general interest. There were of course, replies. What follows is a sample of this "two-way flow". It is included in this chapter because it casts considerable light on the personality and thought of Charles Hartshorne and also has an important bearing on the understanding, and evaluating, of Whitehead's philosophy.

The material is as follows:

(a) Letter from C.H. dated September 1, 1938 concerning my "Bidney's Spinoza and Whitehead". (A copy of this discussion note has been added to this chapter as Appendix A.)

(b) Letter from C.H. dated July 13, 1945 concerning some issues raised by my "The Psychology of Alfred North Whitehead". (I provided the relevant passages on which Hartshorne comments, as Appendix B of this chapter.

(c) Letter from C.H. dated September 7, 1945 in
reply to one from me which unfortunately is
missing. However, the content of his letter
is very significant and it is obvious what
issues are under discussion. It would appear
that my letter included some information (i.e.,
report of conversation with Whitehead concerning
the consequent nature of God) which was later
published in 1969 as "Whitehead As Teacher and
Philosopher" (Philosophy and Phenomenological
Research, Vol. 29, No.3; see Chapter 2 of this
volume).

(d) Letter from C.H. written in early 1967 concerning
the manuscript of my "Whitehead As Teacher and
Philosopher".

(e) Letter from C.H. dated May 20, 1977 concerning my
"The Status of Whitehead's Process and Reality
Categories" and my reply dated July 18, 1977 plus
further comments.

(f) Postcard from C.H. dated December 3, 1979 in which
he indicated that he did not object to my use of
some of his letters to me (which I had previously
identified) in a project dealing with the philosophy
of Whitehead.

Charles Hartshorne
Department of Philosophy

Sept. 1, 1938

Dear Johnson,

I thought at the time Bidney's was a singularly bad article, probably ought not to have been published. But together with your answer it is perhaps worth while. I have never felt Whitehead did a very good thing in the way he brought Spinoza in. For all I can see creativity as the one form or idea is simply all the eternal objects as one. Or, it is the Primordial Nature of God as capable of partial embodiment in finite creatures. Still, it is hard to express it that way too. The scholastic way of treating "being" is closer. God is Being, yet by participation other things have being also. Whatever it is creativity is not an individual, a substance in the proper sense; it does not exist in and through itself, but in the created occasions.

Maybe you know something for Kroner. He is a pretty literal Hegelian, and that is awfully out of fashion. Students don't know what to make of it. But he is a learned, enthusiastic, ingenious, and very charming man.

Sincerely,

Charles Hartshorne

93

July 13, 1945

Dear Johnson,

Thanks very much for the last paper, psych. of Wh. It is a remarkably thorough survey, and I am happy it appeared in a psychology journal.

I wonder a little about one or two of your remarks.

To say that events which are past do not exist may seem equivalent to Whitehead's saying that they have perished. But I have always thought even that was dangerous language. For he also holds that they "live forevermore." True, this is in God, but then as he says elsewhere the truth is simply the unification of all things in the Consequent Nature, so if they live forevermore there then the truth about them is they do not perish or cease to exist. Now one might quote the business about God saying what can be saved, and about transmutation in God. But these expressions are a bit cryptic at least, and the flat saying that it is "without any loss of immediacy" seems to me to have priority as more definite, along with the "immortality of events." Of course from my controversy with Ely you already know about what I could say on this. But to me the great discovery of Bergson, Whitehead, Montague, first of all Bergson (and Peirce) is that precisely past events are existent, the present being merely the most complete of the events which exist, the one inclusive of all the others.

Similarly when it is said that not all elements in the datum event are objectified, this must be carefully interpreted. In one place it is said that only some elements are explicit or effectively present, or something like that. But note the same is true of actualities as wholes; some of them are not effectively present either. So I suspect that the sense in which all actualities are objectified is the same as that in which all their elements are so. There are gradations of relevance, but not absolute non-relevance for any actuality or any element.

94

Your interpretation of the externality of contemporaries as meaning that they have not yet ceased to exist or are not yet completed and so cannot be objectified is not clearly justified to my sense, though maybe it is all right. My objection is very definite, and it is that one of these events, say on a distant star may very well have been objectified in another event on that star, both of these events being our contemporaries. Now how can you say that the earlier of these events is not yet completed and ready for objectification?! You remember that in a passage in Adventures W. says that the limitation of influence to the past as in relativity physics may not apply to mental prehensions (telepathy, I take it), though it appears not settled by the passage whether this influence is merely faster than the speed of light or actually instantaneous, thus establishing world simultaneity perhaps.

By the way, can you judge what Northrop is getting at in his reported discussion with Einstein (Schilpp)? I can hardly imagine W. being so naive and ignorant as N. seems to make out?

Always pleased to hear from you.

Charles Hartshorne.

Charles Hartshorne
Route 2, Box 151
Chesterton, Indiana

Sept. 7, 45

Dear Johnson,

Your letter is very valuable.

On one point I must have been unclear. I
think I meant to grant that W. both said and meant
to say that objectification, other than in God is
negative with respect to some of the eternal
objects ingredient in occasions objectified. My
point was that he ought not to have said or meant
this. I do not recall how far I tried to show
that, even on his own terms, he ought to have
limited "abstractness" of objectification to faint
relevance, rather than zero or negative relevance.
The question is this: since all the feelings of
an occasion are "particular", inseparable from
their subject, and this subject is the total
satisfaction, how can you eliminate elements and
still have that individual satisfaction. In
other words, there seems danger of W's falling into
the doctrine he rejects, that only universals are
prehended. I wonder if I'm right about there
being this difficulty with the "elimination"
thesis.

To tell the truth I am baffled anyway by
negative relevance, which still seems to be
relevance, not really zero.

Your other main point, about God, does not
imply any failure of clarity in my letters. I
did really think that, in spite of the pronouncements to the contrary, W. must on the whole mean
to say that in God all is preserved. And here
you have corrected me. It seems impossible you
should, on the basis of such careful questioning
of W. be mistaken. But here, even more strongly,
I feel that he ought to say the other thing, the
thing he sometimes does seem to say. For one
function of God (expressly affirmed twice, and I

96

think essential to theology) is to constitute "the truth", or the "impartial nexus". To say elements of the past are not in God is to make something beyond God the measure of reality and truth. What? Everything is somewhere including the past as it really was.

Your interpretation, accept by W., means that God is in no sense omniscient or "perfect in knowledge" (except of his own past) unless one argues that to know together all that can be known together ("can be saved") is perfect knowledge. But here I have another difficulty. Why cannot all actualized elements be known together? Since all are together in the past as it actually was they cannot be incompatible, non-compossible. Or should what God doesn't remember be denied reality as past? But then what is meant by its elimination, "it" being nothing? This is Mead's paradox in Philos. of the Present. I am startled to find it is Whitehead's paradox too! But I'm glad to be made to face the truth about W's state of mind-- as I think, confused state. Of course, he says, "we cannot conceive the unification . . . in God.

I agree with your interpretation as to Contemporaries also. But here too have doubts as to the tenability of the doctrine. Relations must be somewhere, including relations of contemporaries. One may say, but they have no relations, there are no relations among contemporaries (as individual). But then there are no contemporaries, for "there are contemporaries" means nothing if not, "occasions co-exist with some other occasions," or "are contained together in some reality which is 'existence now'."

Have you an idea how the Consequent Nature fits into the Contemporary world?

Another puzzle: how does God's present have an epochal character, and if so how does it compare with the creatures'? My hunch is, it has the length of the shortest (so God can experience every real distinction). There is a similar problem about, say, our specious present in relation to longer and shorter ones. Is this anywhere discussed?

As to God being a society, what you report makes W. and my humble self in agreement God's society is <u>analogous not univocal</u> with others, for just the reason W. gives, or its <u>unique completeness</u> of memory for its past occasions. All predicates of God are analogies and W. would have done well to affirm a revised doctrine of "analogy"--revised so that in spite of all difference <u>something</u> is really common, or if you will, univocal. Any analogy involves an abstract identity. Also <u>all</u> analogies are destroyed if concepts are held independent of process.

Thanks so much. I hope for more bait.

Yours

C.H.

Dear A.H.J.,

You seem to prove me wrong in taking W. to
assert omission or negative prehension even in God's
prehensions. I retain my view this is a mistake on
his part, but it does seem deliberate.

Interesting are the many signs that W. knew he
was not wholly clear and consistent, about God for
instance. He said something like this to me much
later. Interesting also the indications that W. was
appreciably influenced by Buddhism, though it still
does not come out that he knew of Buddhism's "no substance" tenet. Peirce, Whitehead, and I have inclined
toward a sort of "Buddhisto-Christian" view, with
varying emphases in the three cases.

Except on the one point referred to above, I'm
not sure that any decisive clarification comes out,
but it's interesting.

I think W. really failed to grasp the aspect of
cogency in the nominalistic arguments. Independence
of particular occasions need not mean eternity in all
cases. Once there are red experiences subsequent
experiences can exhibit similarity in sensory quality
to these earlier ones without having to embody an
eternal redness. And the initial red experiences
could have been replaced by other particular experiences equivalent in that qualitative aspect but
otherwise different. W. never really argued with
nominalists. I think DeW. Parker, Price, and others
have shown that similarity will go a good way to
displace identical elements, especially for a Whiteheadian since there is always identity anyway, the
previous exemplifications being immortally present,
identically there ever after.

So on this point the issue seems as it was.

I am also still not certain that W. always thought
the same about, e.g. whether or not God omitted
aspects. But I certainly see my interpretation of
his meaning as made considerably less probable by
your testimony.

I'm pleased he realized that his denial that God is a personal sequence of AE's conflicts with the Superjective Nature. That alone would cause me to reverse the denial. I also note that he is cautious about denying personality to God. On the whole I am, I confess, slightly encouraged in my presumption that I have thought these topics out more thoroughly than he did.

If the primordial nature is conceptual and the consequent physical, then the concrete divine reality is not just the two together, but rather the de facto divine state of AE, which is not a mere nature but a particular exemplification of the two natures. A nature is one thing, an AE quite another, and two natures together are still just a complex eternal object. Moreover there are new hybrid prehensions in God even if no new purely mental prehensions. Or so it seems to me just now.

If any changes are to be made on pp. 14, 30, 50 (lines indicated above) write me please to that effect. I'll then send the essay back to Farber recommending publication. I hope the length won't discourage him.

How's everything?

Charles.

March 20, 1967

Professor Charles Hartshorne,
Department of Philosophy,
University of Texas,
Austin, Texas, U.S.A.

Dear Charles:

I have just received word from Marvin
Farber that he proposes to publish my "Whitehead
as Teacher and Philosopher" in his journal. I
greatly appreciate your assistance in this matter.

I received recently from University Micro-
films, Ann Arbor, Michigan, a statement to the
effect that they had during the past year sold
six copies of their Xerox edition of Whitehead and
the Modern World. You will recall that this was a
project in which Victor Lowe, you and I colla-
borated. The royalty figure for the six copies
was $1.70. The cheque made out in my name
has been cashed. I am herewith sending you my
personal cheque for one-third of that amount, to
wit, 57 cents. I sincerely hope that this will
not place you in a higher income tax bracket.

With kindest personal regards,

Very sincerely yours,

"A.H."

A.H. Johnson.

AHJ/w
Enclosure:

101

CHARLES HARTSHORNE
724 ·Sparks Avenue
Austin, Texas   78705

May 20, 1977

Dear Johnson,

I recommend your essay for publication, little
as I agree with your conclusions. You do a scholarly
job of stating your case, which is one with which
many will agree.

I think you simply commit the fallacy of mis-
placed concreteness, and that it is really a fallacy.

The problem is to know what concretely individuality, unity, relation, change, are. Anyone can
acknowledge them abstractly. But what are they
given as? is the question. In what sense is a stone
given as one entity? Leibniz faced this question
and gave the answer Whitehead gives. If physics is
right, the stone is not a single entity except in
the sense in which a crowd is so.

As to direct experience Whitehead has two answers
to you:

1) All qualities given in experience, e.g.,
the color of the stone, are qualities of feeling and
so given (my sensation book was in this vein). Thus
the stone is given (subtly not obviously) as a matter
of feeling, not at all as mere insentient matter. In
conversation Whitehead said this was his view. See
A.I. Ch. 14, Sec. vII.

2) Direct experience is indistinct as to details
and individuals. This is what "transmutation" is all
about. The indistinctness is itself given in principle, as can be shown in various ways. Democritus
shrewdly guessed this indistinctness long ago, and
neither physics nor psychology have refuted him. You
do not refute him. You merely assert.

102

Similar remarks apply to your talk about the persistence of self-identity. Whitehead's defining characteristics of the society does that job but treats it (rightly, as all Buddhists have always held, along with Hume, James, etc.) as an abstraction. Concretely there is a new actuality each moment (small fraction of a second). Here too you expect a distinctness about introspection that neither psychology nor physics nor any cogent philosophical reasoning I know of justifies.

So I think you are in error, but deserve a hearing. You defend your case well. I am for the essay. I trust it will be published.

C.

July 18, 1977

Professor Charles Hartshorne,
724 Sparks Avenue,
Austin, Texas 78705

Dear "C.H."

I was very pleased to receive your letter of May 20, 1977 which was postmarked July 5, 1977.

I greatly appreciate your attitude to my paper on Whitehead's categories as expressed in your letter and your recommendation to Farber. He has decided to publish it.

As to the critical points you raise in your letter: (a) I entirely agree that one should seek the concrete meaning of individuality, change, etc. I find a stone to be one entity with many parts, but careful observation does not indicate that it is composed of feelings. With all due respect, I must say that when Whitehead and you refer to the color of a stone as a "quality of feeling" I think you are not reporting direct experience, but rather are expressing a theory-- and employing the term "feeling" in a highly abstract and technical sense. (b) Your comment that direct experience is indistinct as to details and individuals is, I find, correct in some cases, not in others. I understand Whitehead's stress on direct ("immediate") experience to imply a careful, educated, enlightened use of such experience. (c) On this basis I find myself aware of an enduring entity (my mind)--not just a series of (society of) entities. I have come across others who share this view. If, as you seem to imply, you have not--I would be glad to send you a few bibliographical items.

It was most considerate of you to write as you did. I am delighted to have this indication of your good health and continuing interest in a former student. I retired (age 65) June 30, 1976. However, the bad habits of a mis-spent youth have kept me busy at the University. An introductory text (Philosophers in Action) appeared this spring. A book on value (Modes of Value) is due this fall. It is dedicated to my sons-in-law and grandchildren--two of the former, three of the latter (a fourth "on the way"). I am also busy with several inter-related articles on Whitehead.

With every good wish,

Sincerely,

"A.H."

A.H. Johnson.

AHJ/pc

In planning this volume it seemed appropriate to ask Charles Hartshorne if he had any objections to the inclusion of some of his letters to me in my proposed volume. His reply is reproduced here.

8 Dec. 1979

Dear A.H.

Yes, go ahead, indicating any omissions. Is it only some of my letters to you?

If "contemporaries" are discussed it may be a view I later gave up . . . . It would be nice to indicate that.

Good luck,

, Charles.

Dec.3
1979

APPENDIX A

A CRITICISM OF D. BIDNEY'S "SPINOZA AND WHITEHEAD"

As a result of a survey of passages in the writings of Professor Whitehead, two of which are quoted at the beginning of his paper, Mr. Bidney is prepared to summarize one phase of Whitehead's position thus: "He [Whitehead] believes that some such entity as process, change, or becoming is the ultimate reality which serves as the bond of relation between the various events or occasions which emerge in time from the cosmic process."[1]

It is true that an examination of the two passages which Mr. Bidney mentions might be expected to lead one to suppose what Whitehead was espousing a Spinozistic Monism. However, reference to other statements, chiefly in Process and Reality, and Adventures of Ideas, as well as an examination of the general tendency of his work, seem to indicate the fallaciousness of Mr. Bidney's interpretation.

In Process and Reality (31) Whitehead, discussing the "Category of the Ultimate", refers to "Creativity" as "The Universal of Universals characterizing ultimate matter of fact". Thus, in broadly Platonic language, "Creativity" is an "idea" (essence or form) which is exemplified (present) in matters of fact (i.e., particular Actual Entities). Conversely, the creative process, whereby one actual entity appropriates data provided by other actual entities, and so constitutes (or creates) itself, is an exemplification of the "form", "Creativity".

That Creativity (Process, Passage or Activity) is not "one fundamental substrate of which all things are modes"[2] is indicated by reference to Adventures of Ideas (303): "Each event, viewed in its separate individuality, is a passage between two ideal termini, namely, its components in their ideal disjunctive diversity passing into these same components in their concrete togetherness. . . . There is nothing in the universe other than instances of this passage (i.e., actual entities) and components of these instances." In short, there is no creativity apart from actual entities. Creativity is a process of interaction (passage) between actual entities (events, occasions).

Indeed, this fact is indicated in one of the quotations on which Mr. Bidney places much weight Process and Reality 10): "Spinoza's modes (actual entities) now become the sheer actualities . . . . analysis does not lead us to any higher grade of reality". It is interesting to note, by way of contrast, Mr. Bidney's statement: "He [Whitehead] believes that some such entity as process, change, or becoming is the ultimate reality". As a matter of fact Mr. Bidney, in expounding Whitehead's position, cannot legitimately apply the term "entity" to "Process". The general activity is not an entity in the sense in which occasions and eternal objects are entities" Science and the Modern World 248).

It is further clear that Whitehead does not intend to posit some underlying substratum to account for the bond of relation between various events". He states: "the process, or concrescence, of any one actual entity involves the other actual entities among its components. In this way the obvious solidarity of the world receives its explanation" (Process and Reality 10).

It may be asked with reference to this attempted correction of Mr. Bidney's interpretation of Whitehead's position (granted that there are passages in his works which support the view that "creativity" is not an entity or ultimate substrate)--What is to be done about the passages which he (Mr. Bidney) has quoted? There are for example the following: "In the analogy with Spinoza, his one substance is for me the one underlying activity of realization individualizing itself in an interlocked plurality of modes. . . . Each event is an individual matter of fact issuing from an individualisation of the substrate activity" (Science and the Modern World, 99). There is also the statement: "The philosophy of organism is closely allied to Spinoza's scheme of thought" (Process and Reality 10).

Indeed, it seems that if these are to be taken literally, and as quoted, they imply that "Creativity" is to be regarded as an "ultimate substrate". It would appear, then, that Whitehead thinks of "Creativity" in two distinct and contrary senses. However, I believe that this conclusion can be denied on the basis of a more careful examination of the passages in question.

In Process and Reality the problem of Creativity is discussed in a more thoroughgoing fashion, than in

Science and the Modern World. I shall refer first to
the passage quoted from the former. Whitehead is
discussing the "Incoherence" which certain philosophies
manifest. He refers to Descartes, who posits two
(three?) substances, although by definition there can
be only one. Whitehead notes, with approval, Spinoza's
reference to One Substance only. Like Spinoza, Whitehead posits only one sort of Metaphysical entity. But
this is as far as the similarity goes. The one real
Substance of Spinoza is replaced, in Whitehead's
thought by many, real, dymanic actual entities (each
of which exemplifies the Universal of Universals--
"Creativity") ". . . the modes now become the sheer
actualities--analysis of them . . . does not lead us
to the discovery of any higher grade of reality"
(Process and Reality 10).

With this, and the preceding discussion in mind,
I think that it is possible to grasp the meaning of
the debatable passage in Science and the Modern World
(99). The ultimately real, for Spinoza, is the one
Substance, God. For Whitehead, the ultimately real
things are actual entities. When he speaks of "each
event as an individual matter of fact arising from an
individualization of the substrate activity (creativity
(Science and the Modern World 99) and states that creativity is a "character which underlies all occasions"
(Ibid. 248) he apparently means that the Universal
(essence, principle) "Creativity" is exemplified (manifest, present) in particular actual entities (i.e., in
the process whereby actual entities are objectified in
each other in the act of self-creation).

Another apparently troublesome phrase (also
quoted by Mr. Bidney) referring to all actual entities
as "the ultimate creatures derivative from the creative
process" (Process and Reality 124) is seen, on examination, to imply Whitehead's basic doctrine that an
actual entity is "causa sui". That is to say, the
creative process referred to is the process by which
an actual entity creates itself. (Process and Reality
135) In this sense also, God may be referred to as
a "creature" or "accident" of creativity. In other
words, God arises through his own self-creative process. There is no external determination. In this
sense his self-creation is an "accident".

Brief reference might well be made to some other
misinterpretations of Whitehead's position. Mr. Bidney

describes Whitehead as starting with infinite, in-
determinate experience--faced with the problem of
accounting for the origin of change and differen-
tiation into finite modes. (<u>Philosophical Review</u> XLV
587)   In this "Potentiality"[3] an "urge" to realize
itself arises.[4]   In the next stage of development
(according to Mr. Bidney) God is conceived not as a
"substrate of events"[5] but is regarded as a purely
"formal principle" Mr. Bidney claims that God as
Primordial (formal) "makes the eternal objects and
events (actual entities) grow together" (588). His
use of the words 'emergent' and 'emerge' (583, 589)
are unfortunate, since they further obscure the issue.
Whitehead really seems to be saying that God does not
exercise any ultimate control in the creation of actual
entities, and that actual entities do not simply "emerge
Actual entities arise by a process of self-creation
(<u>Process and Reality</u> 135--a passage to which Mr. Bidney
refers). While it is true that in God's Primordial
nature all Eternal Objects are organized in proper relevance, yet those Eternal objects which are actualized
in a particular Actual Entity, are selected by that
actual entity itself. Finally (according to Mr. Bidney)
in "the fulness of time" God becomes actual. To his
formal abstract nature are added concrete data from
other actual entities.[6]   It might be further noted that
Mr. Bidney's usage of the term "consciousness" in describing God's Consequent Nature (590) is non-Whiteheadean.
For Whitehead, "consciousness" arises in a situation,
when relevant and irrelevant possibilities are considered
with reference to a fact--i.e., when fact is confronted
with alternatives. (<u>Process and Reality</u> 409)   Finally, in
opposition to Mr. Bidney's imputation of "no causal efficacy" to God (when actual),[7] it is to be recalled that
God, as an actual entity, has as much causal efficacy as
any other actual entity. That is to say that God provides
"data" for the Physical Prehension of other actual entities, and his Primordial nature embodies the realm of
possibilities (eternal objects) which provide a "lure"
for newly arising actual entities.

   The long paragraph just preceding is an attempt
to indicate the fallaciousness of Mr. Bidney's effort to
show that, in Whitehead's opinion, actuality arises from
possibility by a temporal process.

It is to be noted that Whitehead does not intend his position to be interpreted in terms of a temporal sequence which "in the fullness of time" produces (an actual) God. He indicates explicitly and implicitly that the metaphysical ultimates: Eternal Objects (including "Creativity", the Universal of Universals) and Actual Entities (including God, both Primordial and Consequent) are at all times present in the Universe. "Metaphysics is nothing but the description of the generalities which apply to all the details of practice" (<u>Process and Reality</u> 19). This, of course, does not contradict Whitehead's claim that individual actual entities arise in the course of a temporal process of self-creation.

Thus in the opinion of the writer,[8] it is evident that Whitehead: (1) does not attempt "to derive the actual from the potential",[9] is not trying "to combine a monistic metaphysics with a pluralistic theory of physics and biology". On the basis of a careful reading of relevant passages in Whitehead's recent books, I can see no reason why he is not justified in saying, "The philosophy of organism is pluralistic in contrast with Spinoza's monism" (<u>Process and Reality</u> 114).

Notes

1 and 2. D. Bidney, "The Problem of Substance in Spinoza and Whitehead", <u>Philosophical Review</u> XLV 583. For convenience a shortened version of the title is ordinarily used, i.e. "Spinoza and Whitehead".

3. Note that this is not Whitehead's usage of the term. He applies it to (A) the realm of Eternal Objects, present in God's Primordial nature; and (B) the "data" provided by actual entities for the self-creation of other Actual Entities (<u>Process and Reality</u> 101).

4. According to Mr. Bidney, who yet paradoxically quotes a passage showing that the "urge" is present not in "creativity" but in God's Primordial nature.

5. God was never so designated by Whitehead.

6. Mr. Bidney seems to forget that God is an actual entity, when he states that all God's consequent nature

amounts to is the fact that "the boundless activity takes on a definite determinate character as the result of the self-creative function of the interrelated events" (590). In short, there is no reference to God as one actual event (entity), among other interrelated events (entities).

7. Though as Primordial apparently God has causal efficacy since he "makes eternal objects and events grow together" (Bidney 588).

8. See also the discussion of the "Ontological Principle" in Process and Reality, and in Miss D. Emmett's book Whitehead's Philosophy of Organism.

9. See Mr. Bidney's summary of his (own) argument, pages 591-2.

APPENDIX B

Herewith are reproduced passages from my "The Psychology of Alfred North Whitehead", The Journal of General Psychology, 32 (1945), pp. 175-212--to which Hartshorne refers in his letter of July 13, 1945. (The number 18 identifies Process and Reality; the number 11 identifies Adventures of Ideas.)

. . . any subject endures for only a relatively brief duration. It is composed of various prehensions. When these achieve unity, then the subject as such ceases to exist, except that as "superject" (18, p. 71) part of its content has "objective immortality" in a succeeding subject. (p. 182)

Another very important assumption made by Whitehead is that every actual entity experiences every other actual entity, which is available for prehension (see 18, p. 66). The fact that some actual entities are not available for prehension is because those actual entities being in process of self-creation have not yet reached the stage where they can provide data for the use of other actual entities. Thus contemporary actual entities happen in causal independence of each other (11, p. 251). Because of this close relationship between actual entities Whitehead is able to deal very effectively with the body-mind "problem." (p. 183)

We find Whitehead stating that in God, as receptive of the content of other actual entities, "there is no loss, no obstruction" (18, p. 524). God exercises a "tender care that nothing be lost" (18, p. 525). Yet he goes on to speak, in a qualifying fashion, of "a tenderness which loses nothing that can be saved" (18, p. 525). There is also the basic principle underlying all objectification, that only part of the content of an actual entity can be objectively immortal in a succeeding one.

> Objectification relegates into irrelevance, or into subordinate relevance, the full constitution of the objectified entity. Some real component in the objectified

112

entity assumes the role of being how that
particular entity is a datum in the experience
of the subject (18, p. 97--emphases mine).

Thus with reference to God, "each novel actuality in
the temporal world contributes such elements to a
realization in God" (18, p. 134--emphasis mine).   It
seems to follow, from the quotations just considered,
that not all elements are preserved in God. (pp. 185-86).

114

CHAPTER 6

OTHER RECURRENT

ERRORS IN UNDERSTANDING WHITEHEAD

This chapter is concerned with four mistaken, or misleading, interpretations of Whitehead's philosophy. They occur because of failure to understand fully the complexity of Whitehead's approach to the universe. In general, they tend to involve over-emphasis on a rationalistic approach, and neglect of the ultimate empirical basis of Whitehead's thought.

The following contentions are examined in this chapter: (1) there are no concrete examples of actual entities; (2) Whitehead develops a <u>process</u> philosophy; (3) for Whitehead the concept of God <u>is a</u> "derivative notion"; (4) without God there is no givenness of the past (in Whitehead's philosophy).

There have been a number of misunderstandings of Whitehead's philosophy. Many of these are dealt with in other chapters of this volume. Some have not been discussed here. Attention has been concentrated on a number of inter-related <u>major</u> themes.

I

<u>Are There Concrete Examples of Actual Entities?</u>

In his <u>Whitehead's Metaphysics: A Critical</u> <u>Examination of Process and Reality</u>,[1] Edward Pols states: "We cannot give any concrete examples of actual entities". This involves, in his opinion, a serious paradox. Pols reminds us that Whitehead terms his position: philosophy of organism. Pols then states that Whitehead "tells us that we must think of the activity of actual entities in terms of such organic categories as aim and feeling." But, according to Pols, there is a shattering difficulty: Nothing that is an organism in the ordinary sense of that term qualifies as an example of an actual entity". This difficulty arises because "organisms are in fact <u>societies</u> of actual entities". (Pols, 6)

115

In seeking to clarify his contention, Pols lists a group of different individual entities: (a) an electro-magnetic occasion, (b) an atom, (c) a molecule, (d) living cell, (e) a man. Of these only the first (an electro-magnetic occasion) is (could qualify as) a Whiteheadian actual entity. The rest Whitehead would regard as societies of actual entities. (Pols 7)

It is relevant to note that the admittedly brief and somewhat cryptic comments on this topic in White-head's Metaphysics are supplemented by Pols in his "Whitehead's Metaphysics--A Reply to A.H. Johnson".[2]

This reply supplies an answer to an obvious question: If an electro-magnetic occasion could qualify as an actual entity--surely you have here at least one concrete example. Pols answer is: This is not a concrete example. It is merely inferred--"on the basis of Whitehead's atomistic bias" (Pols Reply 478).

Pols is quite prepared to admit that Whitehead refers to "individual moments of experience". Indeed, says Pols, Whitehead likens actual entities to such occasions of experience; but it is not a case of such occasions being examples of actual entities. It is merely a case of metaphor, not example. Pols then reiterates his now familiar theme: All concrete examples--physical things or entities, real feelings, moments of consciousness however evanescent, organisms --fail as examples of actual entities, however adequate they may be as examples of societies.

Pols is particularly anxious to emphasize the claim that: "No ordinary organism can qualify as a Whiteheadian actual entity " (Pols' Reply, 478).

Pols contends that his Whitehead's Metaphysics is a critical examination of Process and Reality. Nevertheless in evaluating Whitehead's philosophy, he has made considerable reference also to Adventures of Ideas and Modes of Thought. A careful examination of these two books, as well as Process and Reality, quickly reveals "the error of Pols' claims".

Pols is wrong in claiming that Whitehead does not regard moments or occasions of experience as examples of actual entities. As a matter of fact, at least some moments, or occasions, of experience are

116

considered by Whitehead to be actual entities. Thus
we find him saying in Process and Reality, p. 65:
"Each actual entity is conceived as an act of experience." "It is a process of 'feeling' the many data,
so as to absorb them into the unity of one individual
'satisfaction'". Likewise in Adventures of Ideas, he
points out that "the actualities of the Universe are
processes of experience" (p. 253). Further, on page
228 of Adventures of Ideas (a page which Pols himself
mentions) Whitehead is referring to the "things which
make up the sole reality of the universe". He then
states: "These individual things are the individual
occasions of experience, the actual entities". It is
also interesting to note that Whitehead begins a discussion of the terms "individual" and "data" in the
context of an occasion of experience, and then proceeds to state that these words "properly apply to
an actual entity" under conditions which he specifies.
(A.I. 227)

   Quite apart from these specific statements that
(some) occasions of experience are actual entities--
there is a good deal of "supporting evidence". Whitehead finds in occasions of experience characteristics
which he notes as distinctive of actual entities.
Thus, for example, he remarks that "an occasion of
experience . . . is an extreme instance at the end of
a scale of these happenings which constitute nature"
(A.I., 237). There is also "occasions of experience
are the really real things which . . . compose the
evolving universe " (M.T. 206). Compare these two
statements with the oft-quoted: "'Actual entities'
. . . are the final real things of which the world
is made up" (P.R. 27). Very significant (as supporting evidence for the claim that some occasions of
experience are examples of actual entities) is the
fact that cases of experience are analyzed in terms
of prehensions (A.I. 227) which, of course, are
characteristics of actual entities. (P.R. 35)

   On the basis of both the direct and "indirect"
evidence offered here--it is obvious that the relation
of actual entities and occasions of experience goes
far beyond "likeness" or "metaphor". In fact, some
occasions of experience are examples of actual entities.

   Next, what of Pols' claim that all of Whitehead's
"concrete" examples are societies (of actual entities)

117

and not single actual entities, and Pols' contention that "no ordinary organism can qualify as an actual entity" (Pols Reply, 278).

A glance at Pols' list of so-called concrete examples leads one to a mixed reaction. Certainly, physical things or entities (except electro-magmetic occasions) are societies (in Whitehead's technical terminology) not individual actual entities. This may also be true of some organisms. On the other hand "real feelings" and moments (occasions) of conscious-ness, contrary to Pols, do qualify as examples of a Whiteheadian actual entity, though not as a society of actual entities. Bearing in mind the fact that for Whitehead at least some occasions of experience are examples of actual entities--we find him referring to various concrete examples of moments (occasions) of experience (in the context of discussion of the relation of past to present). We recall, for example, the case of a man experiencing anger because of some factor in his environment. (A.I. 235) There is also the familiar illustration of a man uttering first "United" and then "States", or "United", "Fruit", "Company" (A.I. 233-34) In Modes of Thought, p. 228 one finds a very detailed illustration.

But there remains Pols' claim that no organism in the ordinary sense (i.e., an ordinary organism) can qualify as an actual entity--thus Whitehead's claim to present a philosophy of organism, in terms of actual entities, involves serious difficulties--indeed a strange paradox.

The term "ordinary" is of course crucial here. In opposition to Pols' denial of the possibility of an actual entity being an organism or vice versa--it is well to bear in mind that Webster's New Collegiate Dictionary points out that there is a biological, and a philosophical meaning for "organism". The latter is as follows: "any highly complex thing, or structure, with the parts so integrated that their relation to one another is governed by their relation to the whole".

It is not difficult to find passages in Whitehead's discussion of actual entities which fall under this de-finition of organism.[4] Indeed, he obviously regards actual entities as organisms, in a perfectly respectable ordinary sense of the term. For example, in Process and Reality (p. 327) Whitehead brings into focus two uses of

118

he term "organism": (a) it may refer to "the community of actual things", (b) it may on the other hand
efer to the fact that "each actual entity itself is
nly describable as an organic process."

As to "ordinary": as Whitehead aptly notes, what
as at one time exceptional, later may become ordinary
n the sense of being familiar, widely used and accepted.
R.M. 65-6, 137-8)

However, regardless of how one used the term
ordinary".--at the end of this somewhat complex dis-
ussion it is relevant to point to Whitehead's statement at the beginning of Process and Reality (p.30):
The ultimate facts of immediate actual experience are
ctual entities, prehensions and nexūs."

II

"Process Philosophy"

It is interesting to observe that while a con-
iderable number of persons refer to the work of
lfred North Whitehead as "process philosophy", he
imself prefers the label "philosophy of organism".
P.R. v) Likewise of significance is the fact that
harles Hartshorne, on occasion, uses the term "neo-
lassical metaphysics". He also suggests "dependent
rigination" as a possible notation.[5] Also relevant
s the fact that Bernard Loomer, a reputed "namer" of
rocess philosophy, now considers that a more suitable
itle would be: "Process-Relational" philosophy.[6]

On the other hand, Sibley and Gunter are quite
atisfied with the label "process philosophy" (S & G,
2).

Regardless of the "title", it is obvious that
hat is (by some) termed "process philosophy" has
haracteristics other than an emphasis on process.

In a very useful Preface to the Sibley and Gunter
nthology on process philosophy, Charles Hartshorne
utlines the three main areas of agreement, and two of
isagreement, found among so-called process philosophers.
n his judgment they agree that, (i) "being is an ab-
traction from becoming" (S & G, 1), (ii) one should

119

avoid extreme (radical) pluralism or monism. (iii) They agree in rejecting classical determinism. However, there is disagreement among process philosophers concerning (a) the issue of psychicalism vs. psychophysical dualism and (b) the issue of theism vs. atheism or agnosticism.

(A)

In view of the complex situation revealed by the preceding comments, it seems relevant to examine, with care, the status assigned to process by Whitehead.

It is obvious that Whitehead voices strong opposition to philosophers (and theologians) who advocate an essentially static view of reality. In Modes of Thought he provides a brief, vigorous, expression of this attitude. He states that unless "advance into novelty" is taken seriously "existence is meaningless. The Universe is reduced to static futility devoid of life and motion" (p. 109). Whitehead's first category of explanation is relevant at this point: "The actual world is a process, and that process is the becoming of actual entities " (P.R. 33). In similar vein, in Adventures of Ideas, he states: "The very essence of actuality--that is of the completely real--is process. Thus each actual thing is to be understood in terms of its becoming and perishing" (p. 354). In like fashion, in Modes of Thought we find him commenting in his Wellesley College lectures: "One main doctrine, developed in these lectures, is that 'existence' (in any of its senses) cannot be separated from 'process'. The notions of 'process' and 'existence' presuppose each other " (M.T. 131).

In Modes of Thought he emphasizes the point that the apparently static timeless realm of mathematics is incorrectly so interpreted. He invites us to consider the statement: "Twice three is six". He contends that this is not a tautology. Rather "twice three" indicates a form (pattern) of process. "Six" refers to completed fact. (See M.T. 125-26) Indeed, in Whitehead's opinion, "all mathematical notions have reference to process of intermingling " (M.T. 127).

Reference to a "world process" should not be misunderstood. Apparently this phrase means simply: the totality of processes of actual entities. (See M.T. 128

However, despite the obvious emphasis on process, thorough examination of Whitehead's total, comprehensive, treatment of the topic (i.e., the nature of things) indicates that the quotations just mentioned above must be interpreted with great care. Thus Whitehead, in his mature reflective Modes of Thought cogently comments, in his section on Activity: "The discussion . . . has run into exaggeration. The essence of the universe is more than process." He explains his point by expressing the opinion that the notion of "reality devoid of process" would not have been accepted by some great men "unless it expressed some fundamental aspect of our experience" (M.T. 137).

Toward the end of Process and Reality, Whitehead emphasises a characteristic feature of his cosmological scheme. There are final opposites. Among these are flux and permanence. He remarks that these opposites are "in experience with a certain directness of intuition" (P.R. 518). The basic point is this: Whitehead does not assign decisive priority to either one of these opposites--permanence or flux (being or becoming). Both are given an honoured fundamental, place in the total scheme of things. They are seen, when properly understood, to be components (aspects) of one unified experience. This point of view is clearly and effectively expressed by Whitehead's comments on Heraclitus' famous "all things flow". He remarks that the fundamental intuition on which this is based is balanced by recognition of the permanence of things, "the solid earth, the mountains, the Egyptian pyramids, the spirit of man, God " (P.R. 318). The unity of these factors (permanence and flux) in one experience is Whitehead suggests, admirably set forth in the first two lines of a "once" familiar hymn. The first line is: "Abide with me" (permanence); the second line of the hymn is: "Fast falls the eventide" (flux) (see P.R. 318, M.T. 73). Specifically, more technically, there is permanence even in an "always changing" world, because there is repetition of various sorts. There is re-enaction of feeling tone, also re-occurrence of exemplification of eternal objects issuing in social order (in Whitehead's technical sense). (See P.R. 50-51, 236-37, 365; A.I. 235-36, 261-62)

Even more crucial is Whitehead's emphasis on forms of definiteness of process. In other words, there are specific patterns, or characteristics, of specific processes. In passing, it has already been noted, that in mathematics there are forms of process. Among the examples he mentions are: addition, subtraction, multiplication. Indeed "twice three" as noted, is a more specific case. In general (in broadly Platonic terms) a form might be available as abstract possibility or present as realized, actualised, pattern or characteristic of some process. (See M.T. 121-25,127, 130, and subsequent discussion of eternal objects.)

It is interesting to note that some of the entities which Whitehead lists as permanent, for example, stones and mountains, are not eternal. In due course they "wear away"--disappear. One is reminded of his distinction in Science and the Modern World between what endures, e.g., mountains, and what is eternal e.g., a colour (121). In Process and Reality, the term "permanent" is applied not only to entities such as mountains which have a termination date, but also to what he terms "eternal objects", which do not have a date of demise.

It is essential to emphasize that in giving examples of permanence, Whitehead does not refer, as many do, to laws of change. Rather he states: "Laws of change are themselves liable to change" (M.T. 130). He reminds us that species may be dominant for a time, then suffer decline or extinction. Civilizations have their day and cease to be. Even "heavenly bodies" pass through various stages. Incidentally, it will be recognized that Whitehead uses the terms process, flux, change, passage, activity, transition as "roughly" synonymous in many instances. (See M.T. 63, 73, 120, 191, 206; S.M.W. 120-23; A.I. 192, 354-55; P.R. 317-18, 518)

The preceding reference to God involves a return to the unity of permanence and flux theme. Here we are not only confronted by the fact that in the actual world are found both flux and permanence. A further fact is brought into focus. One actual entity, i.e. one of the components of the universe--in this case God --is characterized by both change and permanence, in fruitful mutually required interrelationship. Specifically, technically speaking--God's primordial nature is unchanging (see P.R. 70) but his consequent nature undergoes constant change as it appropriates data from the world of finite actual entities. (See A.I. 357

urther, finite actual entities are not cases of pure
rocess--as noted earlier, there are forms of process.
peaking technically, eternal objects are essentially
nvolved in the life of any actual entity. As White-
ead aptly puts it, "the things which are temporal
rise by their participation in the things which are
ternal " (P.R. 63).

In discussing the details of relations of God
nd the finite actual entities of the world, Whitehead
irmly develops his "unity of permanence and flux"
heme. And thus he states that there is a very complex
ituation. "There is . . . actuality, with permanence
equiring fluency as its completion; and actualxty with
luency, requiring permanence as its completion " (P.R.
27). God's primordial nature requires completion by
he development of his consequent nature by relations
ith the world of finite actual entities. They come
n their sequence, cases of fluency--achieve a partial
ermanency as they are objectively immortal in the life
f God. (See P.R. 527-29)

A further comment concerning the process-permanence
ssue is in order. So far discussion has focussed
hiefly on the actual world and God. As has been noted,
n passing, Whitehead's cosmology also takes into con-
ideration the realm of the possible--specifically the
ealm of abstract possibilities, i.e., what he terms
ternal objects. When they are exemplified in the world
f actual entities they are cases of forms of definite-
ess--and so contribute to the actual world (as noted
reviously). The further, crucial point is this: when
ot exemplified, the realm of eternal objects, in its
wn right, constitutes a factor of permanence in the
niverse. It will be recalled that in commenting on
is categories of existence, Whitehead remarked that
actual entities and eternal objects stand out with a
ertain extreme finality" (P.R. 33).

In order to "round out" this brief discussion of
hitehead's emphasis on endurance (i.e., permanence)
eference must be made to his theory of societies of
ctual entities. This will serve to expand and clarify
he cryptic reference to social order earlier in this
hapter.

Unlike finite actual entities which have a brief
ife span (they quickly arise and then perish)--as has

been pointed out--God does not suffer this fate, nor
do eternal objects. In addition to these bases of
permanence (endurance), Whitehead claims that there
are some groups of actual entities, so related that
they have at least some common characteristics. This
is so because, on their own initiative, the same eternal
object is exemplified in each entity. Thus there is a
sequence of actual entities such that, despite their
individual distinctiveness, a common actualized characteristic has at least a degree of endurance of permanence. Such a sequence of actual entities constitutes what Whitehead terms a society. In this
sense a society is a basis of permanence--despite, or
indeed in the midst of, the process of rise and de-
parture of individual actual entities (see P.R. 365 and
A.I. 260-63).

In the interests of comprehensiveness, it is
important, as well, to realise that on occasion Whitehead not only focussed attention on the "process-
permanence" issue--but also suggests an equally balanced
approach to process and relations (see A.I. 192; M.T. 92
He also notes the mutual "pairing" of process and individuality, and refers to the "erroneous notion of process
devoid of individualities" (M.T. 132). Also highly significant is the comment: "The whole understanding of
the world consists in the analysis of process in terms
of the identities and diversities of the individuals
involved " (M.T. 135).

(C)

The status of process in Whitehead's philosophy
comes into clear focus when one takes seriously his
claim that actual entities are "the final real things
of which the universe is made up" (P.R. 27). Category
of explanation X states: "The final analysis of an
actual entity discloses it to be a concrescence of
prehensions, which have originated in the process of
becoming " (P.R. 35). In other words, process is not
an ultimate underlying subsistent or existent reality.
It is a factor involved in (a characteristic of) what
is ultimately real. It is crucial to note that in most
instances, Whitehead regards it (process) as only one
of several such factors. Thus, for example, when he
refers to "the four stages constitutive of an actual
entity," he mentions: data, process, satisfaction,
decision. (P.R. 227)

An analysis emphasising some variations in terminology, but expressing roughly the same point of view--is found in Modes of Thought. Here he proposes to explain the nature of any existing thing in terms of data, process (with form relevant to the data) and issue. (M.T. 126-27) Strangely this analysis follows, by a few pages, an earlier one using many of the same terms, which is presented as an analysis of process. The factors mentioned are: data, form, transition, issue. (M.T. 120)

Regardless of Whitehead's apparent ambiguity in using the term "process"--it is obvious that his discussion is set in the context of an analysis of actual entities.

In any case, the crucial point is this: In emphasizing process, Whitehead is concentrating on a specific type of process. He is not concerned with process in general. He is not dealing with some sorts of process. Rather he is concentrating on the sort of process which has a number of distinctive characteristics. Thus he states that an actual entity "is a process of 'feeling' the many data, so as to absorb them into the unity of one individual 'satisfaction'". (P.R. 65--emphasis added) Speaking with greater care, Whitehead states that this does not mean that all available data are appropriated. There is selection--hence elimination--loss. (P.R. 363-64, 517; A.I. 255-56) In this psychologically oriented context, Whitehead explains that an actual entity is a "subject". It is an entity "constituted by the process of feeling, and including this process. The feeler is the unity emergent from its own feelings " (P.R. 136. See also P.R. 176). Several clarificatory details should be noted: (i) A subject has self-enjoyment of its process of development. (See M.T. 205-6) (ii) This process of development is one of self-creation. (M.R. 207) (iii) The process is guided by its tendency toward a final goal. (M.T. 207-8)

In view of the status of process in Whitehead's philosophy, it becomes obvious that one should not consider the label "process philosophy" as completely satisfactory--even as a convenient abbreviation notation. If the term "process" is used, might it not be more appropriate to include it in a more comprehensive phrase such as: "Process and Permanence" Philosophy. There is much to be said in favour of the name "Prehensive Philosophy" or "The Philosophy of Actual Entities".

indeed, increasingly one might be inclined to think that Whitehead's own preferred phrase "Philosophy of Organism" is superior to any available alternative.

(D)

The preceding comments on the status of process in the philosophy of Whitehead, provide the basis for an examination of an essay by James K. Feibleman: "Why Whitehead is not a Process Philosopher".[7]

In it he correctly concludes that "permanence occupies as prominent a place in his system as does change or process" (F. 58). However, very strangely, toward the beginning of the essay, Feibleman contends that Whitehead gives a "slight edge" to permanence. He goes even further and states that Whitehead "intended permanence to be dominant over change" (F. 50).

Looking into this issue in some detail, we find that Feibleman having pointed to Whitehead's obvious stress on the factor of process in the world, proceeds to concentrate on the factor of permanence. He calls attention to the realm of eternal objects (F. 52) and to the primordial nature of God (F. 53). He notes also that in the process of actual entities there are elements of permanence (F. 52). However, having made his points, Feibleman does not go on to expand or to explain even in a minimum degree, how this can occur, for example by referring to Whitehead's theories of objectification or society.

Feibleman makes much of his own argument that the structure of the universe is a factor of permanence, i.e., in the universe are found for example: actual entities, eternal objects, prehensions, and so on. In reply, one might object that the "permanence/process" has to do with the nature of the ingredients of the universe. In any case, Whitehead makes it clear that he regards his proposed analysis of the structure of the universe as not completely adequate--i.e., his categories are said to be tentative. Further, the entities thus mentioned are not regarded by Whitehead as having the status: permanent. They may very possibly be replaced by others. (P.R. 139; M.T. 130)

Of very great significance to Feibleman is the claim that the "permanence" interpretation of Whitehead

126

s well supported by the (reputed) fact "that there is
, second set of permanences other than those discussed
.bove unacknowledged and unrecognized", by Whitehead.
F. 58; see also pp. 56-7) Here Feibleman is on very
haky ground indeed. The illustrations he uses do not
upport his contention Whitehead's discussion of
ternal in distinction from endurance and change (in
cience and the Modern World, 121), likewise his treat-
ent of God's functionings, fall well within the clear
ontext of his regular metaphysical system. They are
ot primarily hints of something mysterious and unrecog-
ized. If Feibleman is only trying to show that White-
ead is struggling to achieve a grasp of the complexities
f the universe--he does not do full justice to this
oint. But the main thrust of his argument takes him
ar beyond that. The reputed unrecognized principles of
hitehead's philosophy are not made any more plausible
y Feibleman's distinction between explicit eternal
bjects and the implicit eternal objects of Whitehead's
hilosophy. (F. 57) In brief, contrary to Feibleman's
uggestion, Whitehead was very well aware of the nature
nd implications of his philosophy. He, however, did
ot claim to know everything about the universe of human
xperience.

Scattered through Feibleman's essay, there are a
umber of strange misinterpretations of some of the
etails of Whitehead's philosophy. In the context of
discussion of the role of process in the philosophy
f organism, he correctly refers to the nature of actual
ntities (including God) using a number of apt supporting
uotations. He then states that eternal objects are
haracterized by change. "The actual entities change
uickly, the eternal objects change slowly, but in both
ere is a continual process of change" (F. 48). It is
rue that an eternal object is sometimes exemplified (it
ngresses into different entities) and sometimes is not
-but eternal objects as such are not characterized by
hange. It seems that Feibleman argues erroneously,
rom change in the process of ingression to change as
ssential characteristic of eternal objects. (F. 51)

It is surprising to find Feibleman equating causal
fficacy with matter and presentational immediacy with
nd (or its contents) (F. 54). Also erroneously he
quates actual entities and material, i.e., sensible
bjects. (F. 48, 52) Likewise one wonders why Feibleman
xpects, or wants, Whitehead to account for the origin
f what is eternal--the universal of universals:
reativity (F. 59).

III

The Conception of God--A "Derivative Notion"?

A

In discussing Whitehead's conception of God, W.A. Christian claims that this has the status of: "derivative notion".[8] He begins this interpretation by stating that "there is no explicit reference to God in the categoreal scheme Process and Reality, Chapter 2 . God "is not specifically mentioned in any of the categories of existence, the categories of explanation, or the categoreal obligations" (C. 288). Rather the conception of God is "systematically introduced" in a subsequent chapter: "Some Derivative Notions".

At this point it is well to remind ourselves of the dictionary meaning of derivative (as for example in Webster's Collegiate Dictionary): derived, transmitted, or educed--hence not original or fundamental.

There are two questions to be considered: (a) Is Christian correct in claiming that Whitehead's conception of God is a derivative notion? (b) Are Christian's supporting arguments sound?

Dealing with the second (b) question first, it should be pointed out that Christian is open to some criticisms. It is true that in Process and Reality, pp. 30-42, where he sets out his complete summary list of the components of his categoreal scheme (the category of the ultimate, the categories of existence, the categories of explanation, the categoreal obligations) Whitehead does not mention the conception of God. However, at the beginning of this same chapter ("The Categoreal Scheme") he singled out for special comment four of his basic notions (i.e., members of the categoreal scheme) for special comment. These are: actual entity, prehension, nexus, ontological principle. In discussing the notion "actual entity" he specifically, explicitly, refers to God. He does so again in discussing the ontological principle. (P.R. 28) It may be objected that these references are brief and really are not "systemic introductions" of the conception of God-- but certainly God is mentioned and referred to.

Incidentally, the reputed "systemic introduction" in the chapter entitled "Some Derivative Notions" might well be criticized as suffering from a serious lack of the quality "systemic"! It concentrates on God's primordial nature and does not deal with the consequent or superject natures.

Christian is, of course, correct in pointing out that God is an actual entity and hence is not an entity outside the range of the categoreal scheme. However, Christian is somewhat misleading in stating that this "scheme gives a rigorous statement of the generic traits of actual entities" (C. 288). As a matter of fact, eternal objects and propositions are not generic characteristics of ordinary (finite) entities (i.e., actual entities).

The crucial question is the first (a) one. Is Christian correct in claiming that for Whitehead the conception of God is derivative?

It is true that in Chapter III of Process and Reality, entitled "Some Derivative Notions", he offers a number of comments concerning God, social and personal order and the extensive continuity. However, as one proceeds beyond the title of the chapter, it quickly becomes evident that Whitehead does not here claim that the conception of God is a derivative notion. To begin with, he is discussing the entity God--not the concept that refers to it. Further, the status "derivative" is not assigned to the entity God but (i) to the other actual entities and (ii) the results of God's function as primordial, in arranging and making available the realm of eternal objects. Indeed, in the first paragraph of this chapter, we find that Whitehead refers to "the objectification of God in each derivative actual entity" (P.R. 46). Concerning eternal objects Whitehead states: "There is always the definite relevance derived from God" (P.R. 46). On the other hand, God is referred to as the "non-derivative actuality" (P.R. 48). Even if it be argued that by discussing various entities (including God) one thereby brings the relevant concepts into focus, thus at least by implication one is discussing concepts, or categories[9] --nevertheless the fact remains that in the chapter ("Some Derivative Notions") there is no basis for claiming that the concept of God is a derivative notion.

The only other sort of reference (other than sorts (i) and (ii) to the status "derivative" in this chapter occurs at the end. Whitehead points out that in his cosmological categoreal scheme he repudiates several notions (assumptions) prevalent in past and present philosophy. These assumptions are that the basic elements of experience can best be described, or understood, in terms of some or all of: consciousness, thought, sense perception. According to the philosophy of organism these three entities are not central (basic). Indeed they belong to the "derivative, impure phase of the concrescence" (P.R. 54). Here again the discussion of derivative entities in Whitehead's chapter "Some Derivative Notions" fails to provide any support for Christian's claim that for Whitehead the conception of God is a derivative notion. As far as the entity God is concerned, it is very clear that Whitehead does not refer to God in derogatory terms, i.e., derivative in the sense of lacking fundamental characteristics. (See P.R. 28, Part V, Chap. 2)

It is interesting to note that in Religion in the Making Whitehead states that God "is an actual fact in the nature of things. He is not there as "derivative from the world" (R.M. 156).

It must, however, be noted in the interests of comprehensiveness of treatment, that in Whitehead's notion of God--there is a sense in which he might be said to have a derivative aspect. This involves the fact that in Whitehead's opinion God's consequent nature is constituted by his relations (positive or negative) to the data made available by other actual entities. In one of his cryptic summary statements at the end of Process and Reality is found "In God's nature permanence is primordial and flux is derivative from the World: in the World's nature flux is primordial and permanence is derivative from God" (P.R. 529).

From this Christian initiated digression, it is clear in Whitehead's judgment God is not derivative in the sense of being inferior in status to any other entry in the universe.

(B)

Christian returns to the issue of the reputed derivative status of the concept of God in an essay "The Concept of God as a Derivative Notion" which he

130

contributed to the Charles Hartshorne Festschrift
entitled : <u>Process and Divinity</u>.[10]

At the very beginning, Christian makes it clear
that he regards the issue as essentially a logical
one. Thus he states: "I shall not be concerned with
the way Whitehead's conception of God may have been
formed in his own mind. I want to study the logical
mode at which the concept makes its first appearance
in his system. So I shall be dealing with a logical
question"--"with the logical structure of his system"
C.2, 181). Christian reiterates the theme that the
term "God" does not occur in the outline of the categoreal scheme. It is interesting to note that he does
admit that "it does occur in the informal preface to
the scheme" (C.2 182). The term "informal" is apparently enough, in Christian's opinion, to banish the
preface from serious consideration--despite the fact
that it occurs in the chapter entitled "The Categoreal Scheme".

In any case, Christian makes a useful point
when he notes that the categoreal scheme as outlined
in chapter 2 of <u>Process and Reality</u> (pp. 27-442),
does not include (mention) a <u>particular</u> entity. More
specifically the categories of existence, the categories of explanation, the categoreal obligations
bring into focus <u>types</u> of entities. The Category of
the Ultimate with its emphasis on creativity, one and
many is again not a case of referring to particular
entities primarily, i.e., distinct individuals, but
rather to characteristics of entities. Christian
aptly remarks "there are no proper names of entities
anywhere in the categoreal scheme" (C.2 183). Christian is correct when he states that "these categories
do not single out any entity as having a function which
any other entity of its type does not have" (C.2 184).
The concept God is excluded from the categoreal scheme
because it refers to an entity which does have characteristics which no other actual entity possesses.
Christian thus concludes that the concept of God,
since it is not introduced into Whitehead's system as
a member of the categoreal scheme--is introduced as a
derivative" notion. (C.2 184)

Christian admits that he is faced with the responsibility for stating exactly what he means by
derivative notion". But before doing so he refers
briefly to the nature and status of Whitehead's

categoreal scheme as he (Christian) understands it.
The theory advocated by Christian, is that the need
for the categoreal scheme is "suggested" by human
experience and the scheme is used to interpret this
experience. However, the categoreal scheme is
essentially "definitions of concepts" (C.2 184). As
Christian very explicitly puts it: "It tells us only
what Whitehead is going to mean by such terms as
'actual entity'" (C.2 185). This is a very strange
interpretation of Whitehead's position in view of
his contention that his categories are descriptive
generalizations which reflect, and hence report,
intuitions of data present in human experience.
(See P.R. 6, 7, 12)

It is relevant here to note that Christian in
the first (introductory) chapter of An Interpretation
of Whitehead's Metaphysics (p.3) refers to. "the concrete experience he [Whitehead] takes as his basic
data". This very significant statement occurs in
the context of his discussion of what he terms
Whitehead's "three sorts of discourse". Christian
contends Whitehead's pre-systematic language is only
appropriate to evoke and describe these concrete
experiences. According to him there is a systemic
sort used by Whitehead to construct the categories of
his categoreal scheme. The post-systematic sort of
discourse occurs when the categoreal scheme is used
to interpret self-experience, nature, art, morality
and religion. This interpretation of Whitehead by
Christian seems to overlook the fact that what he
(Christian) terms pre-systematic language is extensively used by Whitehead to interpret self-experience,
nature, art, morality and religion. Also, and more
surprising, as noted above, Christian does not seem
to grasp properly the relation between Whitehead's
categoreal scheme and the concrete experience which
Christian correctly identifies as Whitehead's basic
data.

In view of the importance of this issue, it is
relevant to call attention to the fact that in my
Ph.D. dissertation, which Whitehead read and discussed with care, the following passages occurred
(p. 121):

"Categories

It is sometimes asked why Whitehead has 8
Categories of Existence; 27 Categories of Explanation;

nd 9 Categoreal Obligations. --His answer is
delightfully simple. He believes that the entities
referred to and the functions described are dis-
overable in experience. These categories are
imply statements of the observed facts. As Miss
mmet[11] aptly expresses the matter: 'It (the table
f Categories) is not a dictatorial or a priori
ssertion of first principles, but a formulation of
eneral ideas which have been wrought out of a long
eries of critical inquiries ' (E. 145-6).

It will have been noted that in the course of
his thesis no separate discussion has been accorded
o the various categories. Illustrations of some of
hem have been noted. After all, the special names
nd numbers which Whitehead applies to the principles
xemplified in the behaviour of the Universe are of
inor importance. The basic matter is to note and
valuate these basic principles, in terms of which
hitehead seeks to do justice to every event which
ccurs."

Let us now examine, in more detail, what,
laiming to be expounding Whitehead's views, Christian
as to say about "derivative notion". According to
im, some such notions arise because we learn from
xperience certain facts which are not conveyed by the
ategoreal scheme. The categoreal scheme is then used
o formulate explanations, or interpretations, of the
mpirical facts--hence derivative notions are intro-
uced into Whitehead's system. For example: Christian
nvites us to consider the derivative notion: extension.
e states that we learn from experience (not from the
ategoreal scheme) there is a definite spatial-temporal
rder. One can then use the concept of actual entity
o interpret this fact, suggesting that some actual
ntities have regions,--and then proceed to the deri-
ative notion of extension. (C.2 186. See also C. 78)
hus, in the context of the dichotomy (between the
ealm of pure definition and the realm of experience)
f Christian's interpretation of Whitehead,--the so-
alled derivative notions are not instances of items
n the categoreal scheme, rather they are additional
oncepts. To repeat, these derivative notions are
oncepts developed by use of the categoreal scheme,
ecause of the new data from the realm of experience--
hey are not presented by or involved in the categoreal
cheme.

Christian proceeds from his discussion of extension, as a derivative notion (also of <u>temporal</u> actual entities) to point out that the conception of God is a derivative notion in a different sense from the ones just mentioned. As in the other instances, he emphasizes that the categoreal scheme does not give us the conception of God. Further, he claims it is not introduced because of the impact of experience, as the concepts of extension and temporal actual entity are. The situation is more complex. Here, the initiating factor is not common facts of experience but rather a "technical" problem--the problem of how an actual entity can have a novel subjective aim. (C.2 187)   The problem does not originate within the categoreal scheme. The problem comes into focus with reference to temporal actual entities. The conception of God is introduced to explain the availability of eternal objects to be used as subjective aims. (C.2 187-89)

It is true that Whitehead conceives God as having, among his many activities, the organizing and making available the realm of eternal objects. However, this does not mean that God is thereby assigned a derivative status in the sense of being introduced later--hence the resultant concept (of God) has inferior status either logical or otherwise to that of actual entity or eternal object. According to Whitehead God and the realm of eternal objects and (some) finite actual entities are <u>always</u> co-present factors of the Universe. <u>None</u> of their relevant concepts have the status derivative because of some reputed "come later" deficiency.

Incidentally, in referring to the concept of God, it is strange that Christian deals with only one function of God, the primordial (i.e., making eternal objects available for use as [objects of] subjective aims by finite actual entities). As a matter of fact, Whitehead conceives of God as engaged in many important activities--as illustrated in the life of Jesus of Nazareth. (P.R. 520; A.I. 214)   The conception of God involves a reference for example, to "a tender care that nothing be lost . . . that can be saved" (P.R. 525) Whitehead also thinks of God as "a great companion", "a fellow sufferer who understands" (P.R. 532). Indeed, Whitehead was expressing (reporting) a number of profound insights (intuitions). Contrary to Christian's claim, Whitehead was not using the categoreal scheme merely to interpret some fact of experience, neither

as he in this aspect of his discussion of God only
olving some technical problems concerning the nature
f actual entities or eternal objects. He was, to
epeat, primarily recording a number of profound
nsights.

Toward the end of his essay, Christian tries
igorously and effectively to clear up some possible
isunderstandings of his contention that Whitehead's
onception of God is a derivative notion.

He points out that Whitehead regards (conceives
f) God (a) as a being who exists necessarily, in the
ense that God has no beginning or ending; (b) God
akes an essential contribution to the existence of
very other actual entity. Christian aptly remarks:
Saying the concept of God is the concept of a neces-
ary being is not the same as saying the concept of
od is a necessary concept." Christian further claims
hat it is true that it is systematically necessary:
ithout it Whitehead's speculative system is incon-
istent, incomplete or both. (C.2, 198)

The last page of the essay is worthy of very
areful consideration. Christian states that in
laiming that the concept of God is a derivative notion
concept) in Whitehead's philosophy, he is not sug-
esting that: the concept of God is of less importance
han the concept of actual occasion (entity), or (b)
hat the actual entity God is less essential than
rdinary actual entities (actual occasions). (Indeed
hristian quotes the passages in which Whitehead refers
o the derivative status of actual entities and the
on-derivative nature of God!) Christian makes it
ery clear that he is not concerned with "the content
f the concept, but only . . . with the logical order
n which the concept is built into the system" (C.2,
03). Related to this is the implication that one
tarts with the categoreal scheme and then later, in-
roduces derivative notions. (C.2, 201)

At this point it is appropriate to engage in
ummary critical evaluation of Christian's thesis--
eiterating previous critical comments and adding
elevant supplementary remarks.

The dichotomy which Christian sets up between
he categoreal scheme, which he claims is the result
f definition, and the world of experience (see C.2,184)

135

--is, as pointed out above, not supported in the context of Whitehead's philosophy. Rather, the categories are statements of, or reflect, basic factors found in experience. (See P.R., 6) The categoreal scheme is a statement of the most general factors of the world found in human experience--the most general types of entities. There are many illustrations of, instances of, the members of the categoreal scheme offered by Whitehead in Process and Reality. God is one such illustration, or exemplicication, i.e., a particular case of that to which the concept actual entity applies. It is interesting to note that actually God is introduced (mentioned) before (P.R. 28) as well as after (P.R. 47, 48, 50, Part V) the specific outline of the categoreal scheme. (P.R. 30-42) This tends to undercut Christian's claim of the derivative nature of the conception of God because the concept is introduced later, i.e., after the introduction of the categoreal scheme. It should be noted that Process and Reality, p.28, includes material which in at least one sense might be termed "a systematic introduction of God". In any case Christian seems on occasion to come close to suggesting that the order of presentation in the pages of a book is an indication of logical priority!

While Whitehead's categoreal scheme states the most general and basic factors, or aspects, found in human experience of the world around us--we are confronted also by much detail and very complex situations. There are numerous concepts which refer to or reflect this. Such concepts are not (as Christian claims they are) developed by using the categoreal scheme to interpret facts of experience, or to deal with problems. It is to be emphasized that concepts which refer to details of the functioning of actual entities, or to complex situations, are simply descriptions of what is involved in a moment of human experience It will be recalled that a moment of human experience is the paradigm case of an actual entity (this volume, pp. 24, 38). For example the concept actual entity applies appropriately to such an event and the concept extension also applies (to one aspect of it). There is no mysterious process of developing a new concept extension from the use of the concept actual entity, when one is confronted by a pulse of emotions (i.e., an actual entity).

To repeat, what Christian claims to be derivative notions are for the most part reports on, or reflections of, what is found in human experience. In some cases, for example the concept of God, they are introduced to

eal with problem situations. But it is essential
> realize that when the conception of God is
ntroduced by Whitehead, it is not the case (as
hristian claims it is) of taking the concept (cate-
ory) actual entity and using it to develop a new
erivative concept in order to attempt to solve the
roblem of the availability of subjective aim for
ctual entities. Rather, it is a case of using a
oncept to refer to an instance of an actual entity
nd describing (indicating) how it differs from
ther actual entities (as well as resembles them).
ndeed, one of these distinctive functions of God,
ccording to Whitehead, is to make available, for
ne use of newly arising actual entities, the whole
ealm of abstract possibilities--technically
peaking: eternal objects. The basis for this
niteheadian doctrine (i.e., conception of God) is
is conviction that it is the life and work of Jesus
f Nazareth which constitutes the paradigm case in-
icating the nature of God. It is true that Jesus
rought into focus of attention the entire realm of
ossibilities both positive and negative. He also
anifests the other functions which Whitehead "assigns"
> God: tender care that nothing be lost that can be
aved; "Fellow sufferer who understands";'The Great
ompanion'" (See P.R., Section V).

IV

ne Givenness of the Past

At the beginning of his "Whitehead Without God"[12]
onald W. Sherburne, claiming to draw on William
hristian for support, outlines what he contends to
e a fair and accurate statement of the orthodox in-
erpretation, or presentation, of Whitehead's treat-
ent of the status of the past, ·in his theory of
ctual entities. (S. 252-54) In the opinion of Sher-
urne this essentially involves reliance on the function
f God. This in turn leads to serious inconsistencies.
hus in Sherburne's judgment, one would be 'well rid' of
nitehead's God. In the course of this essay he offers
ther reasons for this conclusion and comments at con-
iderable length on the relevant neo-Whiteheadian views
f Hartshorne and Cobb (and much less fully on those of
gden). Sherburne also sketches his own version of how
> revise Whitehead's philosophy. He considers not only
ne problem of givenness of the past but also has much
> say concerning subjective aim and eternal objects.

137

I propose here to concentrate exclusively on
an examination of what Sherburne terms "the orthodox
interpretation of Whitehead (. . . expounded by
William Christian)" (S. 252)--concerning the givenness
of the past.

It is strange to find that Sherburne, having
vowed to "draw on" Christian "heavily"--apparently
partly misunderstands his approach to the givenness
of the past. After correctly reporting that Christian
points out that Whitehead does not consider it necessary to prove that the past is given, Sherburne then
says that according to Christian, Whitehead 'assumes'
the obvious fact that the past is given (S. 254)--and
asks how this can be. As a matter of fact Christian
reports that Whitehead accepts the obvious fact that
the past is given now. (C. 320)

However, the crucial issue is the question as to
how the past is given now. Sherburne and Christian
remind us that to ask for reasons brings into focus
Whitehead's Ontological Principle: "Actual entities
are the only reasons" (P.R. 37). So to answer our
question as to how the past is "given now" we must
turn to some actual entity (or entities) which serves
as the ontological ground for the givenness of the
past now. Sherburne invites us to join him and Christian in considering how a prehending entity, i.e.,
one now engaged in the process of concretion, i.e.,
actual entity A can prehend a past actual entity: X.

It is pointed out, that in Christian's opinion,
the past actual entity (occasion) X cannot function
as the required ontological ground. This is so because
X has perished and is now no longer actual. (C. 321)
Also it cannot be the newly rising actual entity A,
because the "occasion for which the data are given
cannot be the reason why the data are given" (C. 322)
Christian also remarks that, in the Whitehead context,
it is very obvious that future occasions and contemporary ones cannot be grounds for the givenness of the
past. (C. 322) There remains only one actual entity
capable of performing the required function--namely God.
More specifically, states Sherburne: "God who prehends
all occasions, has prehended X . . . God presents to
A . . . an aspect of himself which includes his prehension of X. In this way the past is given to A to
prehend " (S. 254).

As a matter of fact (a) Sherburne does not give
n accurate report of Christian's treatment of the
heory that God alone accounts for the givenness of
he past. (b) Further, and much more important, both
herburne and Christian are incorrect in what they
laim to be an exposition of Whitehead's discussion
f the givenness of the past now.

Let us consider point (a) first. It is true
hat Christian examines the possible theory that
hitehead's God is the ground for the givenness of
he past, but he states: "In his [Whitehead's] more
etailed and rigorous discussion of causal objecti-
ication there is scarcely a hint that he is even
ware of the problem. Nor is there in these passages
ny explicit introduction of God as the ground of
ivenness" (C. 324). If one turns to less rigorous
assages, "once again this interpretation goes far
eyond the explicit meaning of the passage" (C. 326).
hen Christian contends that because Whitehead failed
o clearly and definitely assign to God the function
f being the ontological ground for the givenness of
he past now--as a result "Whitehead's theory of
ctual occasions is incomplete".

If anyone seeks to assign the "God is the sole
round for the givenness of the past" theory to White-
ead on the basis that even if he does not explicitly
xpound it, it is at least implicit in some passages
n Whitehead's work--two comments are in order. First,
t is admittedly difficult for some ingenious "seekers
or implications" to restrict such activities within
easonable limits. However, secondly, and crucially,
s a matter of fact the claim that one cannot account
or the givenness of the past (within the context of
hitehead's system)--by reference to past actual cases
-is simply to misunderstand what Whitehead means by
ctual entity (occasion).

It will be recalled that Sherburne and Christian
laim that a past actual entity cannot be the ground
or the givenness of the past because it is no longer
ctual--and in order to provide, or be, a ground it
ust be an actual entity. This line of argument ne-
lects the full range of Whitehead's treatment of
ctual entities. According to Whitehead, an actual
ntity is a moment of experience (feeling) which arises
nd achieves unity by a process of taking in some avai-
able material (data), guided by a subjective aim (pur-
ose). Having completed the process of becoming, it

139

perishes. (See for example P.R. 33-39, 336, 364) In
so doing it makes available data for the use of subsequent actual entities. Thus it is of the very nature
of an actual entity that it provide data for the use of
other actual entities. Since the "making available of
data" involves the demise of the source, hence it is
past as far as the present self-creative activity of
the present actual entity is concerned. In this sense
the past entity contributes to the present.

Because of the stated position of Sherburne and
Christian, it seems advisable to provide here a few
representative quotations from Whitehead's writings
concerning the nature of actual entities.

There is, for example, a somewhat technical
passage in Process and Reality, pp. 479-80 (which in-
terestingly Christian himself quotes at length) in
which Whitehead remarks that a present actual entity
(occasion) B prehends past occasion A "as an antecedent
subject as prehending a sensun with an emotional intensity. Also B's subjective form of emotion is con-
formed to it's subjective form". Whitehead accounts
for this by saying that there is "vector transmission
of emotional feelings of a sensun from A to B" (P.R.
479). In this way, says Whitehead, B feels both the
sensun and the emotional (subjective) form as derivative from A. In brief, a past actual entity A provides
data for presently arising actual entity B--or to use
Sherburne's and Christian's notations, past actual
entity X is the ontological ground for the givenness
of the past to the present actual entity A, now in
process of concretion. Thus it is that Whitehead
states, concerning any actual entity: "Its own con-
stitution involves that its own activity in self-
formation passes into its activity of other formation"
(A.I. 248).

The immediately preceding quotations are, after
all, a variation of, or clarification of, Category of
Explanation XXXI (P.R. 38): "The functioning of one
actual entity in the self-creation of another actual
entity is the "objectification of the former for the
latter." Relevant also are Category of Explanation
IV ("It belongs to the nature of being that it is
potential for every becoming") (P.R. 33) and Category
of Explanation VIII (in which he points out that an
actual entity requires two descriptions: one in terms
of its process of becoming--the other concentrates on

140

its potentiality for objectification in the becoming
f other actual entities" (P.R. 34).

Whitehead's views are further clarified on the
ssue of the ontological ground for the givenness of
he past, in his analysis of actual entities in terms
f subject and superject--or more accurately: subject-
uperject.

He states that actual entities have both subject
nd superject aspects. The subject aspect is the self-
irected creative process of being (i.e., the becoming)
unity of experience. The second function of an
ctual entity then occurs. It provides data for the
se of other actual entities and thus has its superject
spect. This involves that the inner life of the
ubject evaporates, it perishes, but as a result data
ecome available for the use of others.

Supporting and supplementing the immediately
receding comments, let us consider some represen-
ative Whitehead "quotations" bearing on this topic.

Of considerable significance is the statement that
n actual entity has a three-fold character: (i) that
given for it by the past", (ii) its subjective charac-
er aimed at in the process of creation, (iii) its super-
ect character namely "the pragmatic value of its
pecific satisfaction" qualifying subsequent activity.
P.R. 134) (See also P.R. 443) In another expression
f this theme, Whitehead remarks that "an actual entity
s at once the subject experiencing and the superject
f its experiences. It is subject-superject, and
either half of the description can for a moment be lost
ight of" (P.R. 43; see also P.R. 71).

It is interesting to observe that in an outline of
he nature of an actual entity, Sherburne "covers"
without correcting his usual general mistake) the two
spects to which I have just referred. Thus he states
hat individual actual entities "are momentary droplets
f experience . . . synthesizing into a fully definite
nity of feeling the elements provided by their environ-
ent . . . they do not linger over their feelings when
ompleted but perish in handing on . . . feelings to
ubsequent generations of actual entities" (S. 253).
hristian also refers, in passing, to the superject
spect of finite actual entities and also of God.
C. 323)

As a matter of fact, Whitehead does indicate that God has a superject aspect, i.e., God provides concrete data (see P.R. 532). As well God makes available abstract data (i.e., the realm of eternal objects). (See P.R. 46, 73, 248)

It is thought by many, though this point is not mentioned by Sherburne and Christian in the material under discussion, that Whitehead involves himself in serious difficulty by claiming that God can, like all other actual entities, make concrete data directly available. In the context of Whitehead's system: objectification involves the demise of the actual entity providing the data. However, God does not die, he does not perish. (P.R. 523-33)

However, Sherburne does claim to discover a serious inconsistency in Whitehead's doctrine. He states that Whitehead having proposed to account for the givenness of a past actual entity X by the functioning of God--then fails to explain how God is able to prehend X--without making God a glaring exception to the basic principles of his system. (S. 265) At issue, as Sherburne sees it are (a) the principle that contemporary actual entities (i.e., those in unison of becoming) cannot prehend each other. (P.R. 95) Thus if God is in process of concretion and an actual entity X is in process of concretion,--then God cannot prehend X. (b) If X is in the past according to Sherburne, since X no longer exists, it cannot be the ground of the givenness of X--hence God cannot prehend it. (c) God being in process of concrescence, cannot be (as previously claimed) the ground for the givenness of the past.

These three principles, according to Sherburne, rule out the possibility of God prehending actual entity X--yet Whitehead contends that God does prehend such an entity and also provides data for newly arising actual entities. (S. 254)

In reply, it should be pointed out that Sherburne is correct concerning points (a) and (c). Nevertheless concerning (b) Whitehead, within the limits of his system, actually does account for the possibility of God prehending X. In other words Sherburne's point (b) is incorrect (see preceding discussion).

Incidentally, it is strange that when dealing with the "no mutual prehensions by contemporaries" theme, Sherburne does not point out that Whitehead is confronted by serious difficulty, namely God, as continually in process of concrescence is said to provide data for the use of other actual entities—also in process of concrescence—i.e., in unison of becoming—thus indulging in a fracturing of basic principles. Here indeed God is treated as an exception to the "usual principles".

It is interesting that in marshalling reasons for being dissatisfied with Whitehead's doctrine of God on the ground of it being an exception to other actual entities—Sherburne did not call attention to the fact that while ordinary actual entities only prehend some eternal objects (P.R. 66)—God prehends all of them. (P.R. 46, 521-24)

We come now to a final comment concerning Christian's approach to the problem of the givenness of the past. It is considered here because while it raises a much larger issue (than is dealt with as a topic of this section of this chapter), nevertheless of has an important bearing on one main concern in this volume.

Christian recognizes that there are passages in Whitehead's writings which appear to marshal some strong empirical <u>evidence</u> in support of the contention that past actual <u>entities</u> serve as sound ontological bases for the givenness of the past. Whitehead claims to find many cases of what he terms "causal efficacy", i.e., the impact of the past on the present. For example: we experience (a) a light causing us to blink, (b) anger from a past experience carries over into the present (A.I. 235-36), (c) feelings originating in the body, or the mind, are felt as coming from these sources in the past, swelling up into the present experience. (M.T. 219-20)

Indeed, in the course of commenting on W.T. Stace's treatment of the "Whitehead versus Hume" analysis of causation, Christian quotes a long paragraph in which Whitehead makes reference to a sense of "derivation from an immediate past" also "sense of . . . influence from other vague presences in the past" (P.R. 271. The reference to Christian is C. 147).

In the face of an appeal to empirical evidence, Christian replies that all this is merely a "pheno-menological account of experience". It is not an explanation of the givenness of the past. It is merely raw material awaiting explanation. As Christian puts it in another fashion: "Whitehead does not intro-duce in this passage his own systematic categories of explanation" (C. 147).

Christian goes further and claims that White-head's answer to Hume concerning causal efficacy "does not consist in pointing out a 'datum' . . . which would validate the causal meaning of our experience". In the context of the "light making one blink" illustration, Christian states that Whitehead does not regard "making" as an additional component of our experience "of the same logical order as 'flash' and 'blink'" (C. 148).

This interpretation by Christian seems strange in view of the passages he quotes from Whitehead (as indicated above) and the "following" references to "derivation" and "influx of influence" (as noted above). If Christian regards "of the same logical order" as an excape hatch, it hardly seems effective. It is signi-ficant that Christian correctly states that Whitehead's answer to Hume "consists in an appeal to experience" (C. 152). Christian states: "Whitehead's account of causal efficacy is not an attempt to demonstrate real connections" (C. 150).

Context seems to indicate that by demonstrate Christian means demonstrate logically. He goes on to say that one can accept the fact of influence or power without having a conceptual explanation, or justifi-cation, for it. This, in Christian's opinion, is Whitehead's position. (C. 150) Christian makes a very significant statement: "Whitehead's own theory of actual occasions, and in particular the mechanism explanatory of causal objectification, is not designed as a sub-stitute for experience. It is designed to make room for the empirically acknowledged fact of influence and to relate it to the general structure of experience" (C. 151).

The preceding several paragraphs "come to a head" in the following very crucial and revealing statement by Christian: "Whitehead takes it as a fact of common experience that the past is given for the present as a real condition imposing the obligation of conformity. But how is it possible, categoreally speaking, that he past which has perished, is given for the present? n an answer to this question, I shall suggest a reason' for causal efficacy. But it will not be a eason in the sense of a logical demonstration that ausal efficacy does in fact take place" (C. 153).

This brings into focus Christian's tendency, on ccasion, to misinterpret Whitehead's approach to his ategoreal scheme. As a matter of fact, Whitehead's asic categories are an expression of a number of asic intuitions of fundamental factors in the world f human experience. Since they state, or reflect, hese factors--their status, in this sense, is econdary. And therefore, on this basis it is strange o find Christian raising the issue of "how categoreally peaking" the past can be given to the present. This s simply a fact of experience. The category "actual ntity" reflects the intuitive fact of experience. here is no categoreal difficulty, as Christian raises t (the past is not actual therefore it cannot provide ata). There appears to be difficulty in this area nly because Christian does not do full justice to hitehead's category. In the context of Whitehead's hilosophy (whatever may be the opinion of Sherburne nd Christian) it is not necessary to account for the mpact of the past exclusively in terms of God's unction, as Christian claims it is necessary to do so.

Christian is in one respect wise in that he does ot attempt a "reason", to show, in the sense of logical emonstration, that causal efficacy does in fact take lace. (C. 153) Finally it should be stressed that hitehead's categoreal scheme manifests descriptive eneralization. Contrary to Christian, its function s not to "make room" for the facts of experience.[13]

Notes

1. Edward Pols, Whitehead's Metaphysics: A Critical
Examination of Process and Reality, Southern Illinois
Press, Carbondale and Edwardsville, Ill. 1967. Here-
after this book will be referred to as Pols.

2. Dialogue, Vol. VII, 1968, pp. 476-78. Hereafter
this item will be referred to as Pols Reply.

3. Webster's New Collegiate Dictionary, G.C.
Merriam, Springfield, Mass. 1958, p. 592.

4. See categories of explanation and categoreal
obligations (P.R. 33-42).

5. See Charles Hartshorne, "The Development of
Process Philosophy" in Process Theology, E.H. Cousins
(ed.), Newman Press, New York, 1971, pp. 47-48.

6. See "Postscript", Process Philosophy, J.P. Sibley,
and P.A.Y. Gunter (eds.), University Press of America,
Washington D.C., 1978, p. 178. Hereafter this book
will be referred to S & G.

7. In Tulane Studies in Philosophy, Vol. XXIII,
pp. 148-59, Tulane University Press, New Orleans,
1974. Hereafter this essay will be referred to as F.

8. William A. Christian, An Interpretation of Whitehead's Metaphysics, Yale University Press, New Haven,
Conn. 1959, p. 288. Hereafter this book will be
referred to as C.

9. As Whitehead seems to do in dealing with social
order. He starts referring to concepts, then goes
on at length to discuss the entities to which the
concepts refer.

10. Process and Divinity (ed. by W.L. Reese and Eugene
Freeman), Open Court Publishing Co. LaSalle, Ill.
1964. Christian's contribution is pp. 181-203. Hereafter this article will be referred to as C.2.

11. D. Emmet, Whitehead's Philosophy of Organism, The
MacMillan Co. London, 1932.

2. Donald W. Sherburne, "Whitehead Without God", _The Christian Scholar_, Volume L, No.2, Fall 1967, pp. 251-72. Hereafter this essay will be referred to as S. It is to be noted that the revised version of this essay appeared in _Process Theology and Chris-tian Thought_, D. Brown, R. Jones, G. Reeves, editors, The Bobbs-Merrill Co. Inc., Indianapolis, Indiana, 1971, pp. 305-28. When relevant references will be made to the revised edition.

13. For detailed discussion of Whitehead's approach to his categoreal scheme, see Chapter 7 of this book, "Intuitions and Categories".

SECTION THREE

CORRECTION OF TWO GENERAL ERRORS

CHAPTER 7

INTUITIONS AND CATEGORIES

I

The categoreal scheme which Whitehead outlined in pages 27-42 of <u>Process and Reality</u> is regarded by some as the central part of his philosophy, its most fundamental ingredient--the foundation on which his philosophy is based. Those who accept this view are guilty of a very serious misunderstanding. As a matter of fact, in Whitehead's judgment, this categoreal scheme is <u>derivative</u>. Specifically, perceptive persons experience a number of basic components (elements) of the world, and of themselves. They then try to formulate a set of categories (general ideas) in order to elucidate these experienced data. In brief, the categories are instruments devised in order to deal with situations confronting human beings. In this sense categories are <u>derivative</u>.

In the first few pages of <u>Process and Reality</u> (before proceeding to outline the categoreal scheme beginning on page 27)--and elsewhere--Whitehead makes his point abundantly clear. He states, in general: "The elucidation of immediate experience is the sole justification for thought.". . . "The starting point for thought is the analytic observation of the components of this experience " (P.R. 6).

In this context, though in another book, Whitehead characteristically refers to "primary aspects of the universe which common sense . . . hands over to philosophy for elucidation " (M.T. 71). More specifically, he points out that the speculative philosophy, (metaphysics) on which he is now about to embark in <u>Process and Reality</u>, is "an endeavor to frame a coherent, logical, necessary system of general ideas in terms of which every element of our experience can be interpreted" (P.R. 4). In addition to (a) <u>interpretation</u>, the categoreal scheme serves (b) to <u>identify</u> and describe basic factors in the world of human experience. As Whitehead states in the second (b) point: these categories are "tentative formulations of the ultimate generalities" (P.R. 12).

In brief, Whitehead is stating that there are <u>basic</u> (primary) factors (components, aspects) in the universe. These are effectively apprehended by intuitions (i.e., process of intuiting). When so apprehended these basic components and aspects (i.e., what is intuited, in this sense intuitions) are identified, described and in many cases interpreted --by general ideas, i.e., categories. If one is in doubt about the validity of any category, this issue can be settled by reference to relevant data which are the focus of intuiting. The data in this sense are intuitions. (Note: dual sense of "intuition".)

It is obviously important to determine exactly what Whitehead means by the process of intuiting and also what entities he claims are intuited (i.e., what he means by: intuition). The Concise Oxford Dictionary states that (in the process sense) intuition means: Immediate apprehension by the mind, without reasoning. In view of some of Whitehead's comments the following alternative terminology might be used: immediate experiencing. However, with very few exceptions, Whitehead uses the term "intuiting" in a somewhat restricted, technical sense. It is a type of immediate experiencing (awareness) which avoids an abstract, partial, prejudiced--hence distorted--approach to what is under observation, or before one. Hence intuiting involves a thorough, balanced, penetrating approach. Thus intuiting is able to apprehend essential characteristics and detect the presence of entities which have been missed by other sorts of immediate experience. (See S.M.W. 122, 276; P.R. 253, 526-27; A.I. 228, 235; M.T. 107)

In this context, intuition obviously is not an esoteric, disreputable technique lacking intellectual respectability. It is a necessary, indeed crucial, part of enlightened and effective experience.

It must be admitted, indeed emphasized, that in many cases intuiting occurs only if a person has a broad background of relevant knowledge and considerable intellectual creativity. One doesn't "grasp" a new important factor in a flash of insight (another term for intuition) unless he is familiar with the sort of situation before him. Some data are not open to the immediate awareness of all men and women. In other words, some intuited data are complex and obscure and come into focus only to a highly trained person who also enjoys, in some cases, an element of what seems like luck. It must be admitted that relevant background information may be marshalled by a process of reasoning.

ut the crucial fact remains. The discovery of new
actors is accomplished by intuition not reasoning--
n some cases.

There are, however, instances where a man who
does not have a specific intuition concerning some
actor, may be led to accept the existence of this
actor by a process of reasoning. For example, Mr. A.
correctly evaluates Mr. X intuitively, i.e., without
benefit of a long process of reasoning. Mr. B may
reach the same conclusion as the result of a process
of reasoning, perhaps making use of a number of facts
pointed out by Mr. A.

It is important to note that an effective process
of reasoning depends on the presence of a number of
acts of intuition. Various steps in the argument must
be "seen" to be logically linked (i.e., apprehended
immediately and directly). The conclusion must also
be seen, directly and immediately, to follow from the
preceding sequence. The whole logical structure must
be seen to be sound.

In brief, the intuiting on which Whitehead relies
is a finding, by immediate awareness of what is actually
present in a situation. It does not depend ultimately
or crucially on propositions involved in a process of
reasoning. The problem of distinguishing sound intuition and what is defective, is an important one and
will be dealt with in more detail later. Suffice it
here, at the beginning of this chapter, to indicate
that Whitehead means by intuition.

II

Whitehead's extensive use of, and appeal to,
intuition in dealing with many major philosophical
problems, will be emphasized by referring to a few
clarificatory examples. This is designed to serve as
background for our major theme, in this chapter
i.e., the relation of Whitehead's categoreal scheme
to the intuiting of some aspects of the universe of
human experience.

By referring to relevant intuitions, Whitehead
makes critical issue with Hume's influential theory
of causation. According to this theory, a person does

153

not have experience of direct connection between so-called cause and so-called effect. Rather, because of experience of past sequences of actually separate and distinct impressions, one forms a habit of expecting them to occur in that sequence. To this Whitehead replies that we do have "direct intuitions of inheritance" (P.R. 253). Consider for example a man who is angry over an extended period of time. During any moment of that experience (except the first) there is a direct awareness (immediate experience, i.e., intuition) of the impact of the flow of anger from past to present moment of experience. (See A.I. 235-36) Likewise, consider the case of a person who says "United Fruit Company" and in doing so feels (i.e., is immediately aware of) guided transition from "united" to "fruit" to "company" (A.I. 234-35). Surely, says Whitehead, there is more than separate and distinct impressions, sequence, habit and expectation. What Hume overlooks is the fact of immediate experience of (intuition of) causal efficacy.

Highly significant is Whitehead's claim that a person can directly intuit one's own mind, own body, and also the external world. (See A.I. 265) Intuition (intuiting) is likewise operative in dealing with the complexities of human social and political affairs. Whitehead points out that a reliance on clear sense data, and in general the techniques of traditional modern science, does not enable us to understand the complexities of United States' national life under Franklin D. Roosevelt in the early days of his presidency--the contribution made by his New Deal Program. A recourse to intuition is required. (See M.T. 185)

Reference has already been made to Whitehead's claim that there are intuitions which are experiences of the external world. In more technical fashion he mentions Galileo's "physical intuition", that is, his intuitions of some basic phenomena of nature, as well as its scientific laws. (I.S. 10) In his famous chapter on "The Romantic Reaction" in Science and the Modern World (pp. 106-23), he commended some of the poets of the period for their intuitive grasp, and discussion of, aspects of nature which many contemporary scientists tended to overlook: change, value, eternal objects, endurance, organism, inter-fusion. In Whitehead's "world view", intuiting is found to extend to aesthetic data and to moral factors. He suggests that without an appeal to intuition, one would not understand the poet's reference to England as: "This precious

154

tone set in the silver sea."(Symb. 67) And consider
is comment that "our intuitions of righteousness
isclose an absoluteness in the nature of things "
M.T. 165). Whitehead expressed a conviction that the
ife and teachings of Jesus of Nazareth are "motivated
y first-hand intuitions into the nature of things"
R.M. 56).

III

Having illustrated Whitehead's extensive reliance
n intuitions in dealing with basic philosophical pro-
lems, we now return to our main concern in this
hapter--the relation of Whitehead's categoreal scheme
P.R. 27-42) to his intuitions of some aspects of the
niverse of human experience.

As has been remarked, all components (elements,
spects) of the universe are data awaiting categoreal
lucidation. At this point it must, in the interest
f clear understanding, be realized that among the
any components of the universe, open to immediate
xperience (intuiting), some are ultimate generalities,
.e., are more fundamental and widespread than some of
he others. Whitehead's categoreal scheme, here under
onsideration, is designed to focus on, i.e., reflect,
.e., identify and describe these ultimate generalities,
nd also interpret them. With this scheme "in hand"
ne can set out to interpret, in this sense elucidate,
omponents which are technically speaking not ultimate
eneralities. The situation is complicated by the fact
hat some of the components of the universe are of
onsiderable importance, but not ultimate generalities.
pecifically, they are not extensively widespread, do
ot occur in very large numbers of cases, i.e., are not
eneral, repetitive, features of the universe as is
he case with so-called ultimate generalities.

Let us now turn to an examination of the basic
primary) aspects (components) of the universe which
he categoreal scheme of Process and Reality, pp.27-42
hould be able to elucidate (as well, of course, as the
ther less important components). Toward the end of
.R. (518), he reports the presence, "in experience
ith a certain ultimate directness of intuition" a
umber of pairs of opposites. These are: joy and
orrow, good and evil, disjunction and conjunction,
. . the many in the one . . . flux and permanence,

155

greatness and triviality, freedom and necessity. We
have already noted the Science and the Modern World
list of poetic intuitions of fundamental aspects of
nature, namely: change, value, eternal objects,
endurance, organism, inter-fusion. (p. 123) Obviously
there is not complete, or exact, duplication in these
two lists. The same is the case with the one that
appears in Adventures of Ideas (pp. 244-45): transient
and eternal, physical and mental, concrete and abstract,
immediacy and otherness, many and one, unity and multiplicity. There is considerable emphasis on the inter-
relatedness of these factors. This is also the case
with the Modes of Thought list which stresses: unity
(oneness) and multiplicity, order and confusion, permanence and change. There are also all the generalities
listed which do not come in pairs, for example, individuality, purpose, and self-enjoyment. In addition to
these lists there are other references to basic aspects
of the universe, some of which are ultimate generalities.
Some items already listed are repeated, sometimes synonymous terms are used.

Consider the following: identity and diversity
(difference) (M.T. 129; R.M. 115; P.R. 32); atomicity
and continuity (A.I. 159, 169); individuality and
continuity (R.M. 88); harmony and discord (A.I. 339);
advance and decadence (A.I. 354); tendency up, tendency
down (F.R. 72); freedom and compulsion (A.I. 28-9), 77,
79, 213); immoral and moral (M.T. 18-20); reality and
appearance (A.I. 268); beauty and ugliness (A.I. 324-25,
330); potential and actual (M.T. 96); subjective and
objective (A.I. 268); finite and infinite (M.T. 108).

In considering fundamental aspects of experience,
one should not overlook Whitehead's contention that
there is a teleology of the universe--the aim toward
intensity and variety.(A.I. 259) Finally we come to
what Whitehead considers to be one of the most fundamental aspects of the universe (along with oneness and
manyness). Specifically, Whitehead found in the universe an aspect (factor, characteristic) which can be
termed "creativity" ("creative advance") in the sense
of novelty. Consider for example: "all things are
involved in the creative advance of the universe. That
is, in the general temporality which affects all things "
(A.I. 183). "The word creativity expresses the notion
that each event is a process issuing in novelty " (A.I.
303).

In the context of his discussion of these basic
aspects of the universe, stressing ultimate generalities,

hitehead constructed his categoreal scheme which he
as outlined on pages 27-42 of Process and Reality.

Whitehead's "Category of the Ultimate" involves
he notion of one (singularity) many (distinctive
iversity) and creativity (novelty). Here there are
bvious references to some of the aspects (components,
lements) of the universe which have just been listed.

When we turn to the so-called "Categories of
xistence" we are confronted by a set of apparently
nfamiliar (with one exception) categories. For the
urposes of this discussion, attention will be con-
entrated on the first six of these categories of
xistence: actual entity, prehension, nexus, subjective
orm, eternal object, proposition. (P.R. 32) It soon
ecomes unmistakenly clear that all of the categories
f existence, except eternal object, "carry" a strong
motional or attitudinal meaning. An actual entity
s thought of (by Whitehead) as a subject, i.e., a
eeler composed of feelings (prehensions) whereby data
re accepted (included) or rejected. Data are feelings,
xcept for eternal objects which are apprehended by
ntellect. Subjective forms are emotional reactions,
r attitudes, to data (except for consciousness, which
evertheless contains an element of feeling). A nexus
s a group of related actual entities. A proposition
as as its subject actual entities, and as predicate--
ternal objects, in a specified relation. The above
utline sketch is based on categories of explanation
10-14, 17, 18, 25, and P.R. 337-39). Category of
xplanation 22 brings out the contention that an actual
ntity is self-created. (P.R. 38) His category of pre-
ension covers relations and change; eternal objects
nd nexus deal with endurance. Each actual entity is
ne and a unity, but there is a multiplicity of actual
ntities and each is different. Hence in dealing with
ctual entities: any actual entity has many diverse
rehensions. There is order in the realm of eternal
bjects and in a nexus by its very nature. Eternal
bjects and propositions elucidate possibility. Actual
ntities are just that: actual.

Categories of Existence 7 and 8, Multiplicity
pure, disjunctiveness of diverse entities) and Contrast
modes of synthesis of entities in one prehension), are
ot discussed here because they are cases of complex
elations of actual entities by means of prehensions.
hey, further, do not have the same degree of importance

157

in Whitehead's philosophy as do the other six categories of existence.

It is clear, from preceding comments, and from a perusal of Process and Reality that Categories of Explanation are an attempt to provide a detailed explanation of the meaning of Categories of Existence. The same is true of the so-called Categoreal Obligations.

As discussion proceeds, reference will be made to the content of these categories--when relevant--as indeed has been done in previous chapters of this book. For example, this has been done in correcting the current misleading interpretations of Whitehead. But it is not necessary to state, in detail, all of Whitehead's categories at this point.

It is obvious that here Whitehead has implemented what he said earlier about the method he proposed to use in his technical categoreal scheme. He has relied on descriptive generalization. Specifically, he has described what he considers to be the ingredients of a moment of complex human experience (P.R. 28)--and then in his theory of actual entities, prehension, subjective form, and so on, has proceeded to generalize, and claim that this description applies accurately to all the modes of immediate experience--i.e., to all aspects of the world of which we are directly aware (intuit).

IV

There are those who "make much of the fact that there is no category God in Whitehead's categoreal scheme as outlined in Process and Reality, pages 27-42. Yet, this is not surprising because God, as discussed by Whitehead, is not an ultimate generality, i.e., not a basic recurrent factor in the universe like oneness, manyness, permanence, change and so on (in other words characteristics which some entities in the universe have). God is one factor present at all times in the universe, not a recurrent one which has many occurrences in a wide ranging fashion. Hence the concept of God is not one of the categories of existence, nor is God mentioned in the general discussion of the categories of explanation or categoreal obligations (outlined on pages 27-42 of P.R.).

It is, however, the case that in more detailed
discussions of the behaviour of actual entities,
references are made to God--as one actual entity in
association with others (See P.R. 28 and Part V) Be
that as it may, in view of the relation of categories
to intuitions, the fundamental question arises: Is
God, for Whitehead, an intuited component of the
universe? In view of what Whitehead says on the importance of basing knowledge on intuition, one would
expect him to claim that there is an intuition of God.
However, as a matter of fact, all through Whitehead's
metaphysical writings from Science and the Modern
World (1925) to Modes of Thought (1938) he does not
claim to have intuition either of the traditional God
or an actual entity God. He specifically states in
Religion in the Making (1926) that there is no direct
evidence (i.e., intuition) for the existence of a
transcendent, creative, personal God.(R.M. 86-87)   In
Religion in the Making he is willing to accept an intuition of "a character of permanent rightness" (p. 61).

In Modes of Thought there is an apparent shift
of position. He mentions "a sense of Deity" (p.140).
Here, obviously, "sense of" serves as a synonym for
"intuition". Some of his comments on deity seem to
be consistent with his theory of God's primordial
nature. For example, he writes: "Deity . . . is that
factor in the universe whereby there is . . . ideal
beyond the actual" (p.140). Further, there is a statement which seems to imply, or to be a rather vague
alternate expression of, Whitehead's theory of the
consequent nature of God. Consider for example: "The
unity of a transcendent universe, and the multiplicity
of realized actualities, both enter into our experience
by the sense of Deity" (M.T. 140).

However these apparent implications and alternate
reiterations of Whitehead's theories of God's primordial and consequent natures--are actually nothing
of the sort. A careful reading of Whitehead's various
references to deity reveals his real meaning. The
following passage is crucial: "The experience of the
deity of the universe" is experience of the ideals--
of ideals entertained, of ideals aimed at, of ideals
achieved, of ideals defaced" (M.T. 141).

Thus, in this context, Whitehead is using the
term "deity" to refer to part of the realm of eternal
objects, i.e., those which are ideals. These, in their

159

relation to actual entities, function as ideal goals
which, when actualized, result in value achievement.
Such eternal objects can be intuited; so can their
realizations. To fully appreciate (i.e., understand)
the deity factor in the universe it is not enough to
merely apprehend value ideals, that is eternal objects.
Further, their relation to the world of actual entities
must be understood. Specifically their function as
guiding principles, lures, ideal possibilities pointing
to values beyond present actuality.

V

Enough has been brought into focus to enable us
to attempt an evaluation of Whitehead's Process and
Reality pp. 27-42 categoreal scheme. The crucial
question before us is: does it provide a set of general
ideas which will enable us to elucidate our immediate
experience? Is it the case that the categoreal scheme
meets the ideal criterion that every entity should be
an instance of one of the categories of existence,
every explanation an instance of one of the categories
of explanation, and so on. (See P.R. 31)

It is essential to realize that Whitehead himself
is a very vigorous critic of this categoreal scheme of
Process and Reality, pp. 27-42. He states that any
categoreal scheme, including his own, suffers from
very serious limitations. Consider for example: "Philosophy can never hope finally to formulate . . . metaphysical first principles (P.R. 6). Hence "metaphysical
categories . . . are tentative formulations of the ultimate generalities" (P.R. 12). This state of affairs
exists, in Whitehead's opinion, ultimately because of
"weakness of insight" concerning ultimate factors of
a metaphysical nature. (P.R. 6) There is a further
difficulty in expressing various insights which we may
have had. We find that our available concepts, and
the language which we try to use, are both inadequate
because of the fact that they are designed primarily
to deal with superficial, rather than profound, matters.
He designates his own speculative scheme as an endeavor
to form "general ideas" in terms of which every element
of our experience can be interpreted" (P.R. 4). He has
no delusions of grandeur. He does not regard his
initial attempt as the final word! Some would find it
strange that he should (did) remark: "If we consider

any scheme of philosophic categories as one complete
assertion, and apply to it the logicians' alternatives,
true or false, the answer must be that the scheme is
false" (P.R. 12). In brief, Whitehead is quite prepared to admit that his categoreal scheme "is very
far . . . from satisfying" the ideals of applicability
and adequacy. (See P.R. 31)

We turn now from general criticisms to specific
ones. Whitehead claims, as we have just noted, that
a speculative scheme would provide a set of general
ideas in terms of which every element in our experience
can be interpreted. The question then to be faced is:
are there elements in immediate experience to which
Whitehead's categoreal scheme (P.R. 27-42) does not do
justice, i.e., does not properly interpret, identify,
describe?

One specific defect of this scheme is a neglect
of some factors which appear in immediate experience--
i.e., the data of intuition. For example, Whitehead
interprets the human mind as a "society"--a series of
actual entities, each having a very brief duration.
According to him, there is no one relatively enduring
entity which has or experiences these data, though the
actual entities are moments of experience. (P.R. 135-36)
A careful examination of one's mental life, unencumbered
by over-simplified metaphysical doctrine, reveals the
presence of an experiencer having, i.e., possessing,
and indeed generating, moments of experience which
Whitehead terms actual entities. This experiencer need
not be interpreted in terms of the ancient theory of
mental substance. (E.R. 60-1, 298, 373-74)

Another instance of neglect is Whitehead's claim
that a complex society of actual entities has only the
qualities of its component actual entities. (See A.I.
260-61) As a matter of fact, careful investigation
brings into focus many qualities which a society as
such possesses, and are not found in any of its component actual entities. Speaking less technically:
many organisms have characteristics which their parts
do not possess.

A very serious defect in Whitehead's categoreal
scheme, here under consideration, is that its categories
do not accurately apply to many ingredients of the
universe. According to Whitehead every physical

object in the universe can be interpreted in terms of
societies of actual entities, i.e., centers of feeling,
self-creative, possessing aim, gradually developing to
a final satisfaction. Yet physical objects in the world
of immediate experience (data of intuition) are not appropriately so described. For example, our immediate
experience of a stone does not reveal the presence of:
feeling, aim, self-creativity, satisfaction. It is not
enough to claim, as Whitehead does, that recent developments in science find phenomena which are what one would
expect, if one endeavored to apply a theory of actual
entities. The fact remains: we do not have direct
experience of affective factors in a stone.

The efficacy of Whitehead's categoreal scheme
(here under consideration) is seriously limited by the
fact that there are a number of inconsistencies in the
meaning of some of his major concepts. Consider for
example "objectification". On occasion it means: the
making available of data by one actual entity for
possible use by another one. (P.R. 82, 230) Yet, sometimes, it means the actual absorption of concrete data
into the life of a new actual entity. (P.R. 32, 38,
134, 517) A similar ambiguity is found in Whitehead's
use of the concept "ingression". Sometimes he means:
eternal objects are under consideration by an actual
entity. (P.R. 82) There is also another meaning:
eternal objects have become fully actualized (realized)
in an actual entity. (P.R. 38, 63, 66)

Whitehead, as he has shown, is well aware of the
difficulties in formulating a categoreal scheme posed
by the inadequacies of language, i.e., lack of suitable
terms to express metaphysical subtleties. Yet he himself, on occasion, seems to introduce unnecessary
verbal complexity and confusion. For example, he uses
the term "feeling" to refer to (1) data, (2) subjective
form, (3) the entire inner life of an actual entity
(P.R. 353-354) So likewise "creativity" is difficult
to understand because of his careless use of language.
As a matter of fact, the concept "creativity", for
Whitehead, is that of a type of novelty which charac-
terizes all actual entities. (See P.R. 339) Yet on
occasion, Whitehead's language is such that he seems
to be saying that creativity is a mysterious entity,
more ultimate than actual entities. He says, for
example: "each individual occasion is transcended by
the creative urge" (A.I. 249); "'creativity' introduces
novelty" (P.R. 31); "creativity achieves its supreme
task" (P.R. 528).

162

In passing, it is interesting and significant to observe Whitehead's apparently "cavalier" approach to at least one of the categories, namely, that of "Conceptual Reversion". He proposes to abandon it, stating that it is no longer necessary once the function of God's primordial nature is understood. (P.R. 382)

VI

In view of the defects of the categoreal scheme (which Whitehead outlined in Process and Reality, pages 27-42)--the question naturally arises: is there an alternate categoreal scheme available? As a matter of fact, Whitehead himself provides and uses one. In the famous "Romantic Reaction" chapter of Science and the Modern World (p. 123) he recommends the use of the following general ideas: change, value, eternal object, endurance, organism, inter-fusion. These ideas are recommended because they refer to fundamental factors in the universe--factors which are among those listed as basic aspects, ultimate generalities. It would seem that Whitehead proposes to deal with the ultimate generalities, not only in terms of highly technical categories and words such as actual entity, prehension, nexus, subjective form and so on-- but also in ordinary, relatively non-technical concepts and terms, such as: inter-fusion, organism, change, endurance, etc.

Let us examine, in more detail, the so-called "ordinary, non-technical categoreal scheme".

Although Whitehead does not specifically do so, these non-technical basic ideas can conveniently be arranged in the following fashion: some of them may be termed either (a) "primary", or (b) "associated"; others may be termed (c) "secondary".

The primary ideas (concepts, categories) are: individual, relation, endurance, change, value, value-opposite. In general, this list is based on a careful examination of Whitehead's use of non-technical concepts. However, it may also be regarded as a revised version of the list he provided in Science and the Modern World, namely: change, value, eternal object, endurance, organism, inter-fusion. Of these concepts, three are sufficiently general, i.e., change, value, endurance. The other three are replaced. The revision consists in avoiding the restricted meaning of organism and replacing it by the more general concept: individual (i.e., one sort of individual is an organism). Likewise since inter-fusion is a specific type of relation emphasized by Whitehead,-- the restricted concept inter-fusion is replaced by the more general one: relation. Eternal object is a highly technical concept. It is dropped from the list. In any case endurance covers an essential aspect of its meaning. The category value-opposite is added for reasons to be indicated subsequently.[1]

It must be borne in mind that each of these primary basic ideas involves other basic ideas which are associated with them in various ways.

With <u>individual</u> are associated: oneness, identity, novelty, diversity. (It will be noted that these implied associated ideas are relational.)

The other primary basic ideas have associates as follows:

<u>relation</u>: In addition to oneness, identity, atomicity, novelty, diversity--other relational ideas, i.e., ideas implied by (covered by) the idea "relation" are: togetherness, order, confusion, many, harmony, disorder, disjunction, conjunction, unity, cause, organism, freedom, necessity[2], finite, infinite, reality, appearance, concrete, abstract, continuity, potential, actual, advance, decadence, subjective, objective; inclusive, exclusive, spatial, temporal.[3]

<u>endurance</u>: permanence, eternal object, immortal.

<u>change</u>: flux, process, mortal, transcient.

<u>value</u>: truth, beauty, good, greatness, importance.

<u>value-opposite</u>: false, ugly, evil, triviality.[4]

Ultimately, a primary basic concept implies another associated basic concept, as indicated, because of the aspects (factors) of the universe to which they refer. For example, as a matter of fact, an individual is one entity and is characterized by identity, diversity and novelty. Among the sorts of relations are: order, confusion, and so on. Cases of endurance are entities which are, for example, permanent or eternal.

Change may take the form of mere flux or a structured process. Beauty and goodness are characterized by value, ugly and evil by value-opposite.

It is crucial to realize that, for Whitehead, the idea individual in all cases implies the ideas: oneness, identity, novelty, diversity. On the other hand, the idea relation does not necessarily imply, in all cases, order or confusion and so on. This is so because while any individual entity is characterized by oneness, diversity, identity, atomicity, novelty--one space relation may be that of order; another relation may be that of confusion and so on. The same general comments apply to the ideas: endurance, change, value, value-opposite (as apply to relation).

The following basic ideas (concept, categories) are also mentioned by Whitehead, but they can be assigned secondary status because they are less general than the six listed above, and are not associated with primary ideas as in the case of other ideas as listed. These secondary ideas are: purpose, self-enjoyment (self-awareness and appreciation), joy, sorrow, physical, mental.

It must be reiterated that the preceding detailed structuring of the so-called non-technical categoreal scheme is not found in the writings of Whitehead. However, its essential features are either stated by Whitehead or implied by his procedures. Any revisions I have made are in accordance with Whitehead's attitude of relying on the results of immediate experience.

In passing, it might be noted that some of the categories (concepts) in the so-called secondary list would have a higher status in Whitehead's technical categoreal scheme, e.g., self-enjoyment, purpose, mental and physical.

It is essential to realize that Whitehead makes extensive use of the categories of this non-technical categoreal scheme in his discussion of various aspects of the universe in general, and of human behavior in particular. In brief, by dealing with basic, ultimate generalities, in ordinary non-technical terms and concepts, Whitehead has provided an alternate scheme of categories (different from the technical ones) which can be used in identifying , describing and interpreting (i.e., elucidating) many of the details of human experience.

It is here suggested that his ordinary non-technical categoreal scheme, in many cases, is superior to the technical one because what is most general and ultimate in the universe, as revealed in immediate human experience (intuition) is not what is referred to by the categories: actual entity, prehension, nexus, subjective form, etc., rather, by what is referred to by such concepts as: individual, relation, change, endurance, and so on. By using the ordinary non-technical categories we are escaping from the restrictive artificiality of trying to describe and interpret everything in terms of one type of entity, specifically some ingredients of a moment in high grade human experience (as interpreted by Whitehead). This over-simplification of attempting to rely on the technical scheme by Whitehead is not justified by appeal to immediate experience. In brief, if one is concerned with the ultimate generalities, individual, relation, change, permanence, are more applicable than actual entity, prehension, nexus, subjective form, eternal object, proposition, and so on.

VII

Whitehead's reliance on intuition, his justification of categories on the basis of intuition, is likely to arouse a strong negative reaction from those who take a "dim view" of intuition. It is customary, in many circles today, to claim that intuition as a purely private, relativistic, procedure is beyond the range of respectable scientific verification or justification or respectability. It is true that Whitehead himself remarks that "the clarity of intuition is limited, and it flickers" (M.T. 69). This being so, why is he confident about intuition? The answer is: Whitehead's reliance is upon carefully controlled, soundly based sorts of immediate experience. Such immediate experience is open to verification by reference to the experience of other competent observers. In discussing religious experience, Whitehead remarks that "what is initially known in secret [private] must be verified in common" (R.M. 138). He points out: that can be done on the basis of the use of symbols--for example, language, whereby a person reports what he is experiencing and finds out whether anyone else is having the same experience. (R.M. 132-33) This approach is, obviously, not

restricted to religious experience as far as Whitehead is concerned.

He is anxious to stress that people vary in
their ability to experience specific entities in
specific situations. For example, some people do not
experience certain types of value, or permanence, or
change (A.I. 379) The situation is this: immediate
experience of some data requires a great deal of
special background experience and training. But,
this being so, the obvious difficulties in obtaining
agreement can be overcome since, in proper context,
there is an opportunity to verify occurrences of
entities, if care is taken to ensure that the situation is proper for effective functioning of intuitive
activity. In any case, is it not true that practically
all persons are directly aware of change, endurance,
and other basic generalities, in some specific situations? In such cases one person can verify his
experiences by reference to those of others. It must,
of course, be emphasized that some of the data intuited
by Whitehead are not subject to verification in a
natural science laboratory (though some are) simply
because they do not fall within the field of natural
science. This, however, in the case of religious and
value intuitions, does not necessarily undermine the
claims of verification. It is here claimed that
actual objectivity is not restricted to areas covered
by the physical and social sciences. Objective religious facts can be directly experienced by a person
who exercises proper care and diligence. The experience
of some people in this field is verified for each by all
others of like mind--just as in the case of physical and
social sciences. Persons avoid errors in science on the
basis of noting mistakes and then avoiding them. This
procedure is open to activities in non-scientific fields.
It is true that in natural science an extensive use is
made of certain instruments of a tangible sort, plus
the instrumentality of mathematics. Such support equipment is not available in other areas of human experience
such as the value and religious areas. However, as
stated above, one can and should avoid sources of error
by first noting them and then figuring out how to overcome the errors, for example, based on prejudice, carelessness, inadequate observation, and so on. This
confidence in intuition finally must be put in proper
perspective. It is surely obvious that it is not here
being claimed that Whitehead, or anyone else, is "right
all the time" in relying on immediate experience. How-

167

ever, there are many instances where intuitive experience seems to be perfectly valid basis for
knowledge claims.

Notes

1. See fn. 4 below

2. This implies the idea of cause.

3. This list of ideas which are associates of relation
is based in part on Whitehead's discussion of the
Category of the Ultimate (P.R. 32) where he states
that implicit in the idea "togetherness" are the
notions: many, one, creativity, unity, diversity.

4. Whitehead discusses "value." and "value-opposite"
under the heading "value". This however blurs a
genuine distinction. The term "value-opposite" is
used in preference to "negative value" or "dis-value"
because of the difficulties involved in these prefixes.
(See E.R. 204-5)

CHAPTER 8

WHITEHEAD'S USE OF HIS NON-TECHNICAL
CATEGOREAL SCHEME

I

Prior to 1925 Alfred North Whitehead's major contributions to the realm of ideas were in the fields of
mathematics and the philosophy of science.[1] Then, with
apparent suddenness, a drastic change occurred: He had
something significant to say about all major areas of
human experience and concern. This became apparent
with the publication of Science and the Modern World in
1925, Religion in the Making in 1926, Symbolism, It's
Meaning and Effect in 1927, and Process and Reality in
1929. The Aims of Education (1929), The Function of
Reason (1929) and Adventures of Ideas (1933) served to
substantiate this point. Modes of Thought (1938) also
had this function, as did "occasional essays" published
in the Atlantic and elsewhere. (See I.S. and W.A.E.S.P.)

Readers of Science and the Modern World were (and
still are) struck by the presence of contrasting chapters, and sections of chapters, characterized on the
one hand by awesome technicality of topic and expression, and on the other by illuminating comment couched
in lucid, even lyrical, prose, congenial to most minds.
The range of topics is also noteworthy; not only are
theoretical aspects of science (ancient and modern)
subjected to careful analysis--the practical influence
of scientific ideas and techniques on the affairs of
men, is also discussed. Philosophic and religious
issues are dealt with in the context of a reference to
modern science. Likewise scientific ideas are supplemented by data from other areas of human experience.
Social reform in general, and educational reform in
particular are discussed. One is overwhelmingly aware
that the author of this book possesses a well-stocked
mind and uses his knowledge with great skill and sound
judgment. There are flashes of sophisticated humor
and "good common sense", and related strong disapproval
of the intellectual foibles of pedants who allow their
theories to blind them to basic facts. The apparently
chaotic "jumping about" in the sphere of the intellect,
is not the sign of a disordered mind. Rather, it indicates the author's awareness of the complexity and
inter-relatedness of "men and things".

In the midst of the examination of a mass of details of all sorts, there is a search for a few basic factors (and hence the ideas which "report" them) in terms of which we can understand ourselves and the world in which we live. The characteristics of Science and the Modern World, which have just been noted, are also found in Whitehead's writings subsequent to this volume.

With the passage of time, and particularly since the appearance of Process and Reality, there has been a strong tendency to concentrate on the more technical, metaphysical, speculative aspects of Whitehead's thought--and hence to neglect Whitehead's views concerning religion, education, social reform, philosophy of history, the nature of civilization. Many of such views are expressed in ideas and language which are predominantly non-technical (i.e., in everyday, ordinary use), clearly expressed and--most have contemporary relevance. In other words, as stated at the end of the preceding chapter, Whitehead developed a non-technical (ordinary) categoreal scheme in which he attempted to provide a valid alternative to the highly technical one outlined in Process and Reality, pages 27-42.

Further, it is not realized that many of his insights in the field of epistemology and ontology (including natural theology) which Whitehead tried to express in terms of his highly technical categoreal scheme and related language--also are conveyed by him, in an efficient fashion, in the concepts and language of ordinary, non-technical communication.

This chapter is designed to indicate the use Whitehead made of his non-technical categoreal scheme in discussing the main areas of human experience, and also its applicability to epistemological and ontological issues. It will demonstrate the fact that Whitehead's main, or only, concern is not with the highly technical scheme of categories and language of Process and Reality, pp. 27-42. More specifically, it will become increasingly obvious that it is absurdly erroneous to assume that what Whitehead did early in his career, namely logic, and later philosophy of science, and finally some highly technical epistemology and metaphysics, is all that is worthy of serious consideration.

We turn now to an examination of Whitehead's use of his non-technical primary basic ideas (individual, change, endurance, relation, value, value-opposite) as he discusses the major areas of human experience and concern. Of necessity, only a representative sample can be considered here. Many details will be omitted except for bibliographical references. In the interest of relatively simplified, and hence manageable presentation, for the most part, the associates of primary basic ideas will not be brought into the discussion.

II

A

From Science and the Modern World onward, Whitehead's concern for the "values of civilized living" is unmistakeable. However, he did not offer a definition of civilization until 1933 when he published Adventures of Ideas. Here he aptly remarked that a civilized man, or society, is characterized by a profound concern for Beauty, Truth and Art. Adventure is a distinctive factor in the life of such an individual or society. Absolutely decisive and essential is the quality Whitehead terms "peace" (A.I. 352-53, 366-67).

This five point definition of civilization arouses several crucial questions, for example: Why is there no reference to theoretical and applied science? Why is moral goodness not included in the list? What is meant by art and peace? Why does art receive such high rating?

A careful reading of Whitehead produces specific answers. Scientific knowledge, for example, can be used or misused with reference to the achievement of the highest values (things valuable). The question about the omission of moral goodness apparently involves serious difficulties for Whitehead. However, it seems legitimate to conclude that he does not intend to downgrade moral goodness. In the definition of civilization he is using the term "beauty" in a very broad sense to include moral goodness and aesthetic excellence. (W.T.R. 113-16) The emphasis on art does not imply an impractical concentration on private factors and hence a withdrawal from the hard facts of life. It is an emphasis on techniques whereby values are brought into clear focus. Refreshment and stimulus for the business of living effectively are obtained.

Thus art involves creative initiative in all phases of human experience. This brings us to a consideration of <u>adventure</u>.

By adventure he means the search for novelty not only, or exclusively, in the physical world but also, and chiefly, in the realm of the mental. More specifically, he is fundamentally concerned with value experience and the expansion of range of such experience He speaks in glowing terms of the great Greek adventurers: philosophers and tragic dramatists. But at the same time he warns against the serious danger of being "backward looking". By all means we should imitate the great adventurers of the past, the ancient Greeks. But the imitation should take the form of emulating their spirit, not slavishly attempting to reproduce the details of their work. (A.I. 332, 352-64) It is in this context that he remarks that "the most un-Greek thing we can do is to copy the Greeks. For emphatically they were not copyists" (A.I. 353).

In terms of basic ideas: change (adventure) is balanced by a stress on <u>endurance</u>--in his notion of peace. As he simply defines it: peace is a "quality of mind steady in its reliance that fine action is treasured in the nature of things" (A.I. 353). The basis of this state of mind, and its fruits, will be discussed while examining Whitehead's treatment of value. Suffice it to say at this point: a person who has achieved the attitude peace, is relatively unshakeable by the impact of stimuli which make most men devotees of St. Vitus.

II

(B)

Whitehead not only renders a great service by providing a clear and adequate definition of civilization at a time when there is much "muddled" thinking on the topic. In addition, he is impressively perceptive in his contention that civilization cannot be achieved (and retained) unless the following conditions are present: respect for the individual person, freedom and tolerance, reliance on persuasion rather than force in social relations,--all activities in accordance with wisdom.

These closely inter-related conditions are discussed at length by Whitehead. He remarks pointedly that unless there is freedom <u>from</u> disease, hunger, death and in general the paralyzing impact of a hostile physical environment--it is pointless to talk about freedom of worship, assembly, of the press. He aptly remarks that there must be a <u>balance</u> between freedom and restraint, even compulsion. He suggests that the problem can be, at least in some cases, solved in terms of membership in a professional group. This <u>institution</u> is the entity in which both freedom and <u>compulsion</u> are vested. (A.I. 77-79)

The priority assigned to persuasion rather than force, as preferred instrument in civil activity, is supported by noting the degrading effect of the use of force--the attendant deterioration of ability to achieve the highest levels of civilized living. "It is the nemesis of the reign of force, of the worship of power, that the ideas of the semi-divine ruler center upon some variation of Solomon's magnificent harem of three hundred wives and seven hundred concubines" (A.I. 108). Be that as it may, this is not to be regarded as a complete denial of the necessity to use force in some extreme cases. However, his crucial point is that when force is used there is a decline from the highest level of civilized living. The preferability of persuasion over force is shown by reference to its employment in family life and in commerce, as ideally envisaged.

Among a number of striking and very effective comments concerning tolerance, the following is typical: "Other nations of different habits are not enemies: they are godsends. Men require of their neighbours something sufficiently akin to be understood, something sufficiently different to provoke attention, and something great enough to command admiration" (S.M.W. 290-91).

The importance of respect for the individual person is a central theme in Whitehead's Philosophy of Civilization. Basically the point is that if there is to be a maximum possible achievement of the defining ideals of civilization, <u>all</u> men (not just some) must have an opportunity to achieve the realization of these value ideals. After all, it is an individual human being who is characterized by adventure, peace and concerns himself with truth, beauty and art. Without such individuals there can be no civilized society.

173

Finally, it is obvious that civilization is the fruit of an effective use of intellect to understand facts and values and then use this knowledge to realize these higher value ideals--and this is wisdom.

It is not difficult to distinguish, in this discussion of conditions for civilization, the so-called primary basic ideas: individual, relation, endurance, change, value, value-opposite.

II

(C)

Whitehead's discussion of specific human activities is set in the context of a well-balanced philosophy of history which emphasizes the same primary basic ideas. He stresses the inter-related function of a number of individual factors: ideas, men, geographical conditions, economic factors, technological developments. He emphasizes both the fact of change and the fact of endurance. He notes with care the value and the value-opposite aspects of any situation. (A.I. Chaps. 1-6)

His discussion of the abandonment of human slavery as a social institution provides a good illustration of his philosophy of history. He notes that the idea of the dignity and worth of an (any) individual human being, serves as a "gadfly irritating and a beacon luring" for many generations. It finally becomes effective when it derives enough emotional charge to arouse people to action. But this is only part of the story. Many men were involved in the formulating of the ideals of human worth, and the need for freedom and tolerance,--also the analysis of the defects of human slavery and the benefits of the life of free men. Here, and elsewhere, he makes excellent use of his extensive historical knowledge and his keen insights concerning social factors. Plato, Aristotle, members of some Catholic orders, Quakers, Methodists and liberal reformers such as Lord Shaftsbury,--all receive favorabl mention--not only for formulating ideas, but also for implementing these ideas. Also, the facts of geography are highly significant. It is easier to dispense with slaves in the envigorating climate of the North than in the enervating temperature of land near the Equator. The invention of labour-saving devices (technology) makes slavery unnecessary. The same is true of some

conomic conditions, for example; the need for highly
killfull free men to take initiative at crucial points
rather than reliance on slaves who are forced to obey
xternal commands only). (A.I. Chaps. 2 & 3)

He makes detailed comments on each one of these
ive factors, considered as such. These are very in-
ormative and have contemporary relevance despite the
act that most of them are illustrated in terms of
istorical references. He suggests, for example, that
very age has a decisive general idea which influences
 large number of more specific ones. The assumption
idea) that human slavery is a necessary basis for an
fficient, even a civilized, society is a case in
oint.

His evaluation of this view of life and his re-
arks that a new form of human slavery is now in
xistence in certain industrial situations (and hence
 new version of the idea) are illustrations of his
mphasis on change and on the factor of endurance as
ell as his concern with the value and value-opposite
haracteristics of the idea of slavery.

The unfortunate results of uncritical assumption,
r acceptance, of the idea of materialistic mechanism
re dealt with very effectively (particularly in
hapter 5 of Science and the Modern World--"The
omantic Reaction"). Here again his emphasis on aspects
f change and endurance, value and value-opposite as
ell as the inter-relatedness of individual ideas--are
ominant features of his analysis.

In discussing men he assigns greater importance
value) to men of reason rather than those who rely on
rute force. The later Hebrew prophets and Jesus of
azareth receive very high evaluation. He is careful
as one would expect) to distinguish what is transi-
ory from what is enduring in their personalities and
ives. He is particularly anxious to remind us that a
great man" cannot function as such unless conditions
re positive. (Here he is emphasizing the importance
f relationship.) (S.M.W. 291-92; A.I. 62-3, 214;
.M. 57)

Whitehead's treatment of technology is unusually
xtensive. In addition to the obvious technology of
aterial objects: roads, engines as the source of power
he deals with the science of navigation and other
echniques in the realm of thought. In other words,

he uses the term technology to cover not only physical instruments but also intellectual ones. Here as elsewhere he emphasizes facts of endurance and change, value and value-opposite. For example it is well to realize that the techniques which were effectively used by enlightened colonial administrators in the 19th century are no longer appropriate. Thus changes have taken place. But the factor of endurance is relevant at least in some situations: There is still a concern on the part of people, of superior character and ability, to assist in the self-development of people who are not yet on a particular level of attainment. (A.I. 33, 95-7, 101, 107; W.A.E.S.P. 56-60, 72)

The significance of geographical factors, i.e., elements of the material environment, receive very careful and perceptive consideration by Whitehead. He "talks" of rainfall and trees, the effects of hills and valleys, and the sea. Recalling his own boyhood, he suggests that a person living in Kent on the foggy shores of the English Channel will likely be characterized by "lonely thoughts",--while a dweller in the beautiful and less stressful countryside around his school in Sherbourne (Dorset) will be more sociable and "sunny" in disposition. (A.I. 6-8; W.A.E.S.P. 95-8, 100, 146, 157)

Throughout Whitehead's writings one finds aphorisms which focus attention on crucial points in a striking fashion, sometimes ironic, sometimes playful, but in any case they catch the eye and stimulate subsequent thought. Consider for example: "As we think, we live" (M.T. 87), "The Egyptians wanted bricks, so they captured the Hebrews" (A.I. 14), "Great ideas enter into reality with evil associates and with disgusting alliances" (A.I. 22).

In the case of social philosophy, he sketches the defects of a narrowly conceived, economically based society--and the sort of reforms required to replace value-opposite by value.

Whitehead's stress on the importance of the individual human being is very obvious in his comments concerning economic factors. He contends that the modern economic system has placed serious restrictions on the freedom of men and women and made it difficult, if not impossible, for most of them to enjoy wide and deep value experience. Employees are forced to spend their working hours in meaningless, repetitious tasks in

176

ncomfortable surroundings,--faced by the threat of
nemployment (and at best, in many cases, forced to
ccept an inadequate wage). To a lesser extent (but
till a very important fact) employers suffer the
ame fate (with the exception of the level of income).
hey must adhere rigorously to the "game plan" which
haracterizes their role in the economic situation.
ll are forced to accept a life which is decisively
nfluenced by the desire for profit and its inextri-
able accompaniment of ruthless struggle as the
ppropriate social relation or reaction. Whitehead is
eminded of the old jingle: "Thou shalt not murder, but
radition approves all forms of competition" (A.I. 39)
here is little or no room for the pursuit and enjoy-
ent of truth, beauty and goodness or any other valuable
ntity. (W.A.E.S.P. 62-78)

In reacting to this value-opposite situation, White-
ead suggests techniques for reform. He outlines ways
n which the economic-political system should be changed
o as to include greater concern for values of civilized
iving. This involves a new sort of economic system in
hich employees have a significant voice in policy de-
isions, i.e., concerning the production and distribu-
ion of goods. Hence there is a genuine place for
ndividual initiative, a situation where working condi-
ions make possible the experience and indeed the pro-
uction of a wide range of higher values (truth, beauty,
oodness). All this requires the presence of a special
ype of business executive. He has no kinship with the
raditional "robber baron" who makes a great deal of
oney at the expense of the misery of many of his fellow
en. In Whitehead's view, the ideal "tycoon" shall not
nly have adequate grasp of all phases of the machinery
f the business, but should also have a genuine concern
or the needs of his employees, and of the other members
f society. (A.I. 112-14, 118-20; A.E. 67-8)

Such a reformed economic system is not an idle
ream. It involves the extension and intensification
f enlightened tendencies now operative in at least a
ew modern industries. The result is, and will be,
ot only improved working conditions for employees and
better pattern of life for them (and employers) but
s well, will provide an environment in which a wider
nge of highly valuable products will be evolved and
de available for the enjoyment of all members of
ciety.

A number of incisive specific comments occur in the course of Whitehead's discussion of social issues. He reminds devotees of change that too rapid "reform" may well destroy what is at present characterized by value, and prevent future value achievement. Effective living involves routine as well as novelty--without the stability of routine there is chaos. On the other hand, opposition to change frequently comes from those who are very comfortable now, and fear that social change will bring about a deterioration of that status. Whitehead shares with Plato (and Marx) the "comment" that standards frequently indicate, or reflect, the interest of the dominant class in society.

Typical of his power of "turning a telling phrase" are the following: "political loyalty ceases at the frontiers of radical incapacity" (A.I. 79); The social-contract theory of the state is very useful, it provided foundations for the American and the French Revolutions and in Britain helped to "dismiss the Stuarts into romance" (A.I. 71). The theory of the sole sovereignty of the State is "a mere stick with which to beat Papists"; "a mere way to provide policemen for the counting-houses of merchants" (A.I. 76).

Whitehead does not hesitate to touch on international problems. Here also he illustrates his philosophy of history and elucidates his definition of civilization. His writings on international relations cover the period from 1925-1942. The plea for tolerance involved in his remark that other nations should be regarded as godsends not as enemies, has already been mentioned. In discussing the importance of friendly relations between the United States and Great Britain, he continually stresses the need to develop individual differences while retaining, and respecting, the common heritage and above all the importance of engaging in active and co-operative inter-action in pursuit of mutually enjoyed values. He suggests that the recent history of the British Empire and Commonwealth provides impressive illustrations of how men of different backgrounds, but with shared ideals, can avoid impending conflict and develop mutual respect. He was particularly impressed by the activities of Ghandi and Lord Irwin in 1931. (A.I. 205; W.A.E.S.P. 136-43)

A

Whitehead's remarks on education and religion
are better known than his more general comments on
civilization, philosophy of history and social issues.
Here again the primary basic ideas are obviously involved.

The following coverage of a representative sample
of his suggestions and criticisms concerning education and religion, will serve to demonstrate their
continuing aptness and appeal, despite the passage of
over 50 years.

Whitehead shows his concern for the individual
by contending that since there are very great differences in needs and abilities of individual persons,
the educational process should be adjusted accordingly.
Above all, efficient minds should not be regarded as
receptacles into which materials are piled, under
external initiative--rather, the human mind is a
developing organism to be stimulated and aided, not
blindly compelled. The activity of learning should
be an experience of discovery by an individual, i.e.,
a process of self-development,--aided, of course, by
the teacher and other factors in the environment. Here
the element of relationship is involved. It is obvious
that for Whitehead, ideally, an educational system
should have teachers who arouse students to emulate
their appreciation and use of knowledge. A great
teacher is so vibrant with imaginative activity that
he (she) makes ideas come alive and so "leads" students
to the same sort of experience. In an ideal educational
situation, ideas are inter-related. The seamless gar-
ment of knowledge is not torn apart into artificially
unrelated "subject" fragments. Further, in the aspect
of relationship; ideas are "mated with action", in
other words put to practical use. As knowledge in-
creases and mind develops, new ideas will come into
focus and also techniques for the application of these
ideas to the solution of human problems. Thus the
factor of change will have an essential place in an
ideal educational system. Yet there are enduring
principles of value available for guidance. Further,
a degree of endurance, i.e., stability, is required,
namely sound habits of thought and action. For
example, consider the scientific ideal of formulating

tentative generalizations on the basis of careful individual observations, subject to later verification by oneself and others. (A.E. Chaps. 1, 7; W.A.E.S.P. 156-76)

In discussing education Whitehead not only has much to say about what is involved in an ideal educational process, and the goal it seeks, i.e., the achievement of civilization. He also stresses the defects of some educational procedures. Some of these arouse in Whitehead "savage rage" because they shatter legitimate hopes, and ruin the lives, of unfortunate students whose individuality is not respected. For example, students are forced to "swallow" meaningless bits of unco-ordinated factual information devoid of practical implications. Obviously this educational milieu does not encourage creative change but rather static drudgery, where the dominant factors are characterized by value-opposite. (A.E. Chap.1)

In dealing with educational issues the "philosophy of history" factors clearly are involved. In discussing the functions of teachers and their operations, the importance of men, ideas, and techniques are being emphasized. An ideal educational system is, of course, the embodiment of a co-ordinated set of ideals. The impact of the economic system has an important effect on educational ideas and techniques. Geography also has a part to play--ideally, Whitehead suggests, a school (i.e., its teachers) should take advantage of the stimuli provided by a specific type of physical and social environment (including both natural elements and those which are the result of human handy work). For example in his native Kent, with the historic invasion beaches nearby, and the relics of various civilizations scattered about--it is easy to encourage a student to develop an interest in history.

Whitehead's examination of education involves a number of comments concerning a university faculty. Care must be taken to select individuals who are good teachers and scholars. But the worth of a faculty depends also on the relations of these individuals to each other. A professor should "wear" his learning (ideas and techniques) with humility. What he knows should be used with creative imagination. He should regard his proper status as that of an ignorant man using his relatively scanty supply of knowledge as best he can for the benefit of all mankind. One important

factor in producing an excellent faculty is the pro-
vision of a favourable environment, physical, social
and economic. Implicit is the ready availability of
techniques required for teaching and research. (A.E.
Chap.7; W.A.E.S.P. 156-76)

Whitehead's discussion of education is particularly
rich in pungent aphorisms which illustrate some of his
main ideas. Consider for example: "The students are
alive, and the purpose of education is to stimulate
and guide their self-development" (A.E. v); "The
second-handedness of the learned world is the secret
of its mediocrity. It is tame because it has never
been scared by facts" (A.E. 79); "Learning preserves
the errors of the past as well as its wisdom" (I.S.
57); "Nothing is more difficult than to distinguish
between a loud voice and vigor, or a flow of words and
originality, or mental instability and genius, or a
big book and fruitful learning" (W.A.E.S.P. 168-69).

III

B

In the field of religion[2] Whitehead's famous
definition "Religion is what the individual does with
his own solitariness" (R.M. 16) is only one example of
his stress on the individual. However, it is balanced
by his equal emphasis on world loyalty, i.e., relation
to other men and to God, Characteristically, Whitehead stresses the fact of, and the need for, changes
in religious doctrine and procedures. But some elements should endure. He is very explicit about the
value and value-opposite characteristics of various
religious doctrines and practices. (R.M. 60; S.M.W.
Chap. 12; A.I. Chap. 10)

More specifically, here as in other major areas
of human experience, Whitehead is concerned not only
with what he points to as the ideal but also with what
he considers to be defective forms of an entity. In
his opinion ideal religion, as has been noted, involves
 stress on the importance of the individual--in particular the purification of his "inner parts", and also
his external behaviour. For Whitehead, formal religious
observances are not essential--namely "authorized"
ecclesiastical symbols, ritual and certain kinds of
emotional reaction. A Christian should attempt to

181

imitate, or emulate, the life of Jesus of Nazareth and implement his teachings. In Whitehead's opinion, Jesus is superior to Buddha, Mohammed and other world religious leaders. (R.M. Chap. 1, 4; S.M.W. Chap. 12)

In the ideal form of religion, one seeks companionship with the sort of God portrayed by "the prophet of Nazareth". Relations with one's fellow men should be based on divine personality traits. Specifically God should be thought of in terms not of overwhelming power, or unsympathetic "morality" or metaphysical ultimacy beyond human understanding--but rather in terms of love, tender care, companionship, co-operativ activity for the achievement of civilization with its adventure in an attempt to obtain peace.

In Whitehead's opinion, God undergoes change. In developing his view, Whitehead considers very carefull the life and teachings of Jesus. For example, regardi change, it will be recalled that as a young lad, it is reported that "Jesus increased in wisdom and stature, and in favour with God and man" (Luke 2:52). The process of development took place not only during his youth, but also subsequently. At the beginning of his adult life, he underwent a process of development in overcoming temptation (Matthew 4: 1-11). At the very end of his life on earth, as he was about to die on th cross, he achieved an increase in insight, and the development of certain personality aspects. It is recorded that he said: "Let this cup pass from me. Never theless not my will but Thy will be done" (Matthew 26: 39).

Such an ideal religion will embody the conditions of civilized living--in addition to respect for the individual there will be freedom of thought and action tolerance, the use of persuasion rather than force-- these fundamental factors in religion will operate in the context of wisdom.

In this respect, Whitehead's discussion of the relation of religion and science is very significant. The relation should not be that of opposition--rather: mutual respect. Each can learn from the other. Religi should accept change in the same tolerant fashion as science does, and co-operate with those with whom one disagrees regarding basic ideas, in an effort to bring about an agreement concerning the truth. On the other hand religion can add data, for consideration, which

are not within the range of science. On this basis
wisdom is manifest. As new ideas and techniques
become available, changes should occur in doctrine,
ritual, ecclesiastical organization and all the other
less obviously religious activities of daily life.
But the truly religious person "holds fast" to what
is of enduring worth in the teaching of its founder--
and in particular his moral and spiritual principles.
The details of moral codes will vary as social conditions change, but the ideals of love and order in
human relations will endure. For example love of
fellow men at one time (under frontier conditions)
seemed to be served by leaving one's door unlocked so
that a weary traveller could help himself if the house-
holder happened to be temporarily absent. Under present
conditions it seems more appropriate to have a recognized agency to look after those in need, supported by
financial contributions and part-time volunteer service
from those who are concerned with this problem.

The relevance of the "philosophy of history"
factors is very obvious in Whitehead's discussion of
religion. The place of men is illustrated by his
comments concerning Jesus of Nazareth. Whitehead makes
supplementary remarks about the Hebrew prophets and
many other religious leaders and groups of men. Ideas
have also been mentioned in the discussion above.
Whitehead's grasp of ecclesiastical history is very
impressive and illuminating as he examines the adventures of ideas in the realm of religion. He has much
to say about the use of words (a form of technology)
in an attempt to formulate religious doctrines. Their
limitations are stressed. Words are designed to deal
with what is relatively simple and common in human
experience. Many aspects of profound religious insights are not adequately covered by presently available
verbal equipment. Consider the fact that religious
documents (including the Bible) are continually being
revised as far as their verbal formulations are concerned. Whitehead offers some interesting suggestions
concerning alternate symbols: odors, geometrical forms,
patterns of light, sounds other than those which are
involved in the spoken word. The geographical factor
is obviously relevant in religion. Where a group of
people live seems to have some bearing on whether or
not they think of the deity in terms of male or female.
Likewise one's ideas of hell seem to reflect what, in
a particular geographical region, constitutes extreme
conditions: either very hot or very cold. As for
economic factors: the famous comment of Karl Marx,

that religion is an opiate for the people, brings into focus the point that frequently downtrodden "nobodies" have a very large place in their lives for religion. Whereas it is, for some highly successful people in the economic sense, merely a formality. As Whitehead puts it: "a decent formula wherewith to embelish a comfortable life" (S.M.W. 262).

As in the case of other topics, a number of "quotable quotes" appear in Whitehead's discussion of religion: "Apart from its religious vision human life is a flash of occasional enjoyments lighting up a mass of pains and misery, a bagatelle of transcient experience" (S.M.W. 268); "Religion is the last refuge of human savagery" (R.M. 37); "Wherever there is a creed, there is a heretic round the corner or in his grave" (A.I. 66); "Religions commit suicide when they find their inspirations in their dogmas" (R.M. 144); "The power of God is the worship He inspires" (S.M.W. 268).

IV

A

We turn now to a very brief consideration of Whitehead's mathematics and his philosophy of science. It is interesting to realize that he is prepared to express some general insights in the field of mathematics in terms of ordinary non-technical categories (concepts) and language. Thus he remarks that an individual mathematical formula is a statement of a relationship and involves change as well as endurance. Obviously there is a concern for the value truth and an attempt to avoid the value-opposite false. (M.T. 123- 25) In his philosophy of science it is worthy of note that his theory of events can be expressed at least in part in terms of the concept change and his theory of objects in terms of endurance.[3] Whitehead makes it clear that he is prepared to wrestle with the problem of relationship, and in individual cases. Here again there is a concern for truth and the avoidance of what is false.

B

It is appropriate, at this point, to be reminded that in the preceding chapter it was pointed out that the data (of intuition) which Whitehead elucidated in

184

erms of his technical categories are also effectively
covered" by his non-technical categories. Indeed it
as suggested that since the non-technical ones were
ore general in application than the technical ones,
herefore they are superior to them--for some purposes.
ore specifically, the technical categories are re-
tricted in range because they are based on an obser-
ation of some aspects of a moment of human experience,
hereas the non-technical categories are not so
estricted. To put it in another fashion, they apply
ppropriately to the many entities which are not in-
redients in a moment of human experience. Specifi-
ally, while the concept individual applies to whatever
he concept actual entity refers to, it has a far wider
ange of application, e.g., to a stone, a cloud, a
ish.[4] Likewise relation has a wider range than pre-
ension (which is restricted to feeling relations).
eaction has a wider significance and application than
bjective form. Endurance is wider in use than eternal
ject or nexus--in Whitehead's technical usage.

V

It is crucial, when discussing the relative status
f technical and non-technical categories and terms, in
itehead's philosophy, to recognize that from the very
eginning he attempts to explain the meaning of techni-
al terms by the use of non-technical ones. For example,
itehead in explaining what he means by the category
tual entity indicates that what this category refers
 are "drops of experience, complex and inter-
ependent" (P.R. 28). He further states that actual
tities are "real, individual and particular" (P.R.
). A fact of togetherness of actual entities be-
use of their relations with each other, is called a
xus. (P.R. 30, 35) Prehensions are defined as
oncrete Facts of Relatedness" (P.R. 32). More spe-
fically, "the 'prehension' of one actual entity by
other actual entity is the complete transaction,
alyzable into the objectification of the former
tity as one of the data for the latter, and into
e fully clothed feeling whereby the datum is absorbed
to the subjective satisfaction" (P.R. 82).

Eternal objects are defined as "pure potentials
r the specific determination of facts", also "forms
 definiteness" (P.R. 32). Subjective form is
plained by stating that it is how a subject (an
tual entity) prehends data. (P.R. 35)

185

Concerning the other categories of existence, Whitehead does not provide very effective non-technical explanations.

However, it will become obvious that he makes a concerted effort to provide explanatory _illustrations_ of the data (items) to which categories of existence refer. For example, in _Modes of Thought_, page 228, there is a detailed description of a moment of human experience. It begins: "I feel myself as essentially a unity of emotions, enjoyments, hopes, fears, regrets, evaluation of alternatives, decisions--all of them subjective reactions to the environment as alive in my nature." He goes on to give an effective non-technical description of most of the main aspects of his theory of actual entities. He explains his category of eternal objects by pointing out that there are entities, apprehended by intellect, which are abstract in the sense that they are not apprehended by sense, and some of them are ideal possibilities such as democracy, honesty. Others are abstract in realms other than value ideals such as mathematical entities, for example, the number 2. He gives several examples of subjective form in ordinary language. Consider for example: emotions, purposes, aversions, consciousness. (P.R. 35).

It is obvious that in explaining the meaning of his categories of existence, Whitehead not only uses ordinary language and concepts, but also very technical notions and verbalizations. However, here again, he makes a strong effort to explain these categories by using ordinary non-technical concepts and terms. For example, the technical concepts "satisfaction" and "objectification" were used in his definition of "prehension". Since actual entities, in Whitehead's opinion, are characterized by a process of development they will have a final phase. This is termed "satisfaction". For example, he states: "It [satisfaction] is fully determinate (a) as to its genesis, (b) as to its objective character . . . (c) as to its prehensions--positive or negative--of every item in the universe" (P.R. 38). Concerning objectification he states: "'Objectification' refers to the particular mode whereby the potentiality of one actual entity is realized in another actual entity" (P.R. 34).

The concept of "concrescence" has a prominent place in Whitehead's metaphysics. He defines it thus: "The 'production of novel togetherness' is the ultimate

otion embodied in the term 'concrescence'" (P.R. 32).
t may well be objected that while some of the ex-
lanatory terms are ordinary, non-technical and rela-
ively easy to understand (such as potentiality,
ealization, definiteness)--nevertheless, the meaning
f some rather relevant statements, which include these
rdinary terms, is not always as clear as one might
ish. In reply, it should be realized that Whitehead
rovides illustrations drawn from ordinary, everyday
xperience which cast considerable light on some of his
ore difficult doctrines and points of view. The same
echnique, of course, is employed in explaining doc-
rines which are couched in almost exclusively techni-
al terms. It must be admitted that Whitehead does
ot proceed in this fashion as often as one might
ish--but careful probing of his writings brings into
ocus a considerable number of very useful, simple,
llustrations which have a bearing on otherwise very
oscure theories.

His theory of the conformation of subjective
orm, from one actual entity to another (thus showing
he inter-relatedness of things), is illustrated by
eference to an angry man, seething with rage, over
period of several minutes. (A.I. 235-36) His theory
 close body-mind relation is clinched by the humorous
emark: Wouldn't it be silly for me to appear at a
ocial gathering and say: "Here am I and I have brought
 body with me!" (M.T. 156). His doctrine of the
rect perception of the external world is illustrated
 a non-technical comment that no young man, "in his
ght mind", is going to analyze an association with
s partner at a dance in terms of: "I experience a
ux of sense data: by jove, I bet there's a young
dy back of that!" (classroom comment).

However, even granting Whitehead's technical
tegories are difficult--nevertheless they can be
plained, after much effort, using concepts and words
 ordinary discourse, aided by reliance on everyday
lustrations drawn from ordinary experience--(all
sed on intuition of basic factors). When this is
e case, they constitute a very valuable instrument
th reference to some data, i.e., those concerning
ich they are appropriate and adequate. It is a
eat saving of effort, and involves greater accuracy,
 use an understood Whiteheadian technical categories
ther than a vast series of ordinary terms and illus-
ations, to make a significant point concerning some

aspects of human experience. In other words, in some contexts the technical categories and words of Whitehead's system are admittedly superior to ordinary ones (despite the fact that they can be explained, after a fashion, in terms of ordinary procedures). Yet, it must be reiterated that there are many cases where ordinary categories are superior to technical ones because a wider range of application is embodied in the non-technical concepts, or the restricted nature of the technical ones simply makes them inappropriate for use in some contexts.

It should be clearly understood that in this chapter and the preceding one, no attempt is being made to provide a complete discussion of Whitehead's metaphysical categories. Rather, the purpose is to indicate the general nature and status of his technical and his non-technical categories and relevant terms (words)   Only supporting data sufficient for this purpose, have been included.

VI

In summary: as we move from Whitehead's discussion of civilization to his treatment of the philosophy of history, to his examination of specific social problems, to what he has to say about education, religion, philosophy of science, mathematics, and metaphysics-- all are dealt with in terms of a small group of non-technical primary basic ideas (and other basic ideas). These elucidate (i.e., describe, identify, interpret) the basic aspects of the universe which any adequate approach to a fundamental human problem must take into consideration. Those ideas constitute a viable alternative to the categoreal scheme outlined in Process and Reality, pp. 27-42. Further, and more generally, Whitehead provides discussions of a wide range of fundamental human problems, which are impressively perceptive and incisive. Most of these discussions, despite the passage of over fifty years, still have "contemporary relevance".

. For example: <u>Universal Algebra</u>, <u>Principia Mathe-</u>
<u>atica</u> (with B. Russell), <u>The Principles of Natural</u>
<u>nowledge</u>, <u>The Concept of Nature</u>, <u>The Prinicple of</u>
<u>elativity</u>.

. This phase of Whitehead's work has had a very
xtensive impact in the form of Process Theology.
ence references to religion are relatively lengthy.

. Alfred North Whitehead, <u>The Concept of Nature</u>,
ambridge University Press, Cambridge, 1920, pp. 167-72.

. It is true that Whitehead attempts to interpret
tones, clouds and fish as: societies of actual en-
ities. But, as far as immediate experience is con-
erned, stones, clouds and fish are not found to be
omposed of centers of feeling, characterized by
ubjective form, etc., etc., hence the concept of
ctual entity, more specifically, society of actual
ntities, does not apply appropriately in such cases.

CHAPTER 9

A "MODEST PROPOSAL" CONCERNING

WHITEHEAD'S THEORY OF GOD

I

Whitehead's theory of God is set in the context
of value judgements concerning various widely held
views on the topic. He deplores, and rejects, concepts which stress such descriptive notions as: blank
mystery (void), enemy, ruthless and merciless moralist,
imperial despot (relying on brute force), abstract
metaphysical first principle, absolute difference from
anything in the world (i.e., wholly transcendent, completely infinite).[1] In contrast, Whitehead is convinced
that God should be thought of in terms of: love, patience,
persuasion, sharing common characteristics with the world,
a great companion, a fellow sufferer who understands,
tender care saving what can be saved.[2]

Whitehead's negative and positive conclusions in
these value judgements "reflect" his insights (i.e.
intuitions),[3] regarding moral and metaphysical issues
in general, with concentration on the life and teachings
of Jesus of Nazareth, in particular.[4]

In examining Whitehead's discussion of God, one
quickly finds that there are several serious difficulties
to be faced. Whitehead proposes to think of God in terms
applicable to any actual entity.[5] Thus we find ourselves
confronted by the awesome, concentrated complexity of the
last few pages of Process and Reality; brief cryptic
remarks scattered throughout Process and Reality, and
other expressions of the "God as actual entity" general
idea, in Adventures of Ideas; and also the earlier
"trial runs" in Science and the Modern World and Religion
in the Making (i.e. discussions of God before the theory
of actual entities was worked out, in detail, in Process
and Reality.[6]

Two very important issues must be faced. First: Is
Whitehead's view of "God as an actual entity" a report
of what is found in immediate (direct) experience? (It
will be recalled that Whitehead stresses that all valid
thought must begin with, and be verified in, the context

191

of immediate experience. P.R. 6.) Second: Does Whitehead's actual entity God do justice to (accurately
elucidate) various moral and religious insights, and
the life and teachings of Jesus?

II

Let us consider first the question: Does Whitehead
claim to have immediate experience of God as an actual
entity? The answer (see discussion, this volume, pp.159-
60) in summary, is as follows: In crucial passages
(in Religion In the Making, Science and the Modern
World, Process and Reality, Adventures of Ideas) he
does not make such a claim. In a key paragraph in
Process and Reality, Whitehead distinguishes between
most so-called "final opposites" which are intuitive
(P.R. 518) and the pair God and the World which are
termed interpretive and hence, apparently, they
are not intuitive. In Modes of Thought, however, he
speaks of "a sense of Deity", (M.T. 140). It is clear
from the context that "sense of" is a synonym for
"intuition" (M.T. 142). However, a careful reading
of the relevant passages, M.T. 110-12, reveals that by
deity Whitehead means: ideal possibilities, i.e., eternal objects of the value type. These eternal objects
are, of course, open to intuition. Likewise, so are
actual entities which involve realization of such eternal objects. However, Whitehead does not claim that
"deity" is a synonym for "God" (as an actual entity).

In any case, it is here contended that one must
reject any claim to have direct experience of an actual
entity God who has organized ideal possibilities (and
other eternal objects), and makes available, all abstract possibilities in the universe for the use of
other actual entities (i.e., what Whitehead terms
"God's primordial nature"). Specifically, we human
beings do not have immediate experience of such a past
activity or present activity by an actual entity (functioning in these very complex fashions). This claim
is in accordance with Whitehead's own theory of actual
entities. (This book pp. 34-35.) In the last analysis,
according to Whitehead, the inner life and function of
an actual entity can only be immediately experienced by
that entity itself. Concerning all other actual entities, only some data made available in the superject stage of an entity (i.e., upon its demise) can be

192

mmediately apprehended by another. (P.R. 38; A.I. 249;
..T. 228; P.R. 126, 222, 336) Thus in the context of
his phase of Whitehead's philosophy, only God can have
irect awareness of God's ingredient component processes.

In brief, in the context of Whitehead's philosophy,
t this point (concerning God), we human beings are
onfronted by an interpretive theory, not an actually
xperienced inner life of an actual entity. It is true
hat we do experience an organized pattern of (some, not
ll) abstract possibilities (eternal objects); but (to
epeat) we do not experience a process of organizing by
n actual entity God, nor the reputed process of making
hem available. Of course, we do have experience of a
uman person confronting us with a range of related
ossibilities.[7] We have reports of Jesus of Nazareth,
ho was very effective in this function. But Jesus was
ot one actual entity. In any case, no one has (has
ad) direct experience of Jesus's inner life. Strictly
peaking, when we have direct experience of being con-
ronted by ideal possibilities (by a person) we directly
xperience only the body of a person, and the symbols he
ses to bring the possibilities to our attention. There
s no direct awareness of a person's mind--which is in-
olved in the process of confronting.

The preceding comments concerning the lack of
irect awareness of an actual entity God organizing and
aking available ideal possibilities--can be paralleled
ith reference to other characteristics Whitehead men-
ions as descriptive of God. Specifically a person does
ot have immediate awareness of an actual entity God
eing patient, loving, exercising tender care--and so
n. However, we do experience some human beings overtly
ehaving in these fashions (i.e., expressing or evincing
hese characteristics). More specifically, it must be
ealized that, for example, love for another person in-
olves not only a specific sort of overt behavior, but
lso specific inner, private emotions (motives) and
ntentions. These (latter two) are not open to direct
bservation by others. Hence there is need for caution
n making claims about our experience of the three
spect type of behavior: love of another person.*

_____

ee A.H. Johnson, Modes of Value, Philosophical Library,
w York, 1978, pp. 50-56.

III

As one reflects on Whitehead's theory that God, in his primordial nature, organizes the realm of eternal objects--a question occurs. Is this a sophisticated version of a point of view which Whitehead usually vehemently rejects--namely that God imposes his purposes on the world (the emphasis on overwhelming power)[8]? Is there an essential difference between an emphasis on God's power, such that the Cedars of Lebanon shake and smoke--and God's decisive initiative in imposing order on the realm of eternal objects? Surely this approach to God is very different from the stress on love, patience, tender care, and so on. The claim of God's absolute control over one very important aspect of the Universe is in striking contrast with the general theory of the persuasive, saving, nature and function of God.

All these comments bring us to the second important issue: Does Whitehead's technical theory of God, in the context of his theory of actual entities, properly interpret (apply adequately to) the data of his moral and metaphysical insights as reported at the beginning of this chapter?

Insofar as God receives data from other actual entities, and makes data available for them--the terms: tender care, love, great companion, even fellow sufferer who understands--in some cases are applicable, but in a very tenuous sense. Likewise since God does not force specific data on any other actual entity, and waits for the demise of other entities before receiving data from them--to that extent the term persuasion and patience apply. However, very serious reservations and doubts arise concerning the adequacy of Whitehead's theory of actual entities when one contrasts the love, tender care, patience, companionship and saving function of Jesus of Nazareth (as described in the Gospels) with the activities of an actual entity--even of a uniquely complex and enduring one--namely the God actual entity of Whitehead's technical theory. A moment of the "feeling life" of a human being (as interpreted by Whitehead), which is the thought model for an actual entity, simply does not have the complexity of function and content of the experience of Jesus of Nazareth (or some of the Hebrew prophets, or a few contemporary persons who approximate his moral and spiritual excellence)--in relation to the world of man and things.

Whitehead is not justified in assigning to the
actual entity God, of his theory, the characteristics
of Jesus of Nazareth--even though the same verbal labels
and very general concepts may be applied in a very tenuous sense. We turn now to an elucidation of these
general critical comments.

A relation between Whitehead's actual entity God
and everything else is either: (1) God confronts these
actual entities with abstract possibilities (eternal
objects) or (2) concrete data (the functioning of his
superject nature) or (3) God absorbs some concrete content from other actual entities and so saves these data
(consequent nature).[9]

A careful examination of the details of Whitehead's
theory of actual entities is very important. In the
context of this metaphysical theory, it becomes evident
that while the actual entity God can provide data (concrete and abstract) for possible use by newly arising
actual entities--once the new entities have achieved
distinctive individuality (i.e., completed their process
of self-development) God cannot have relations with them
as such. They immediately go out of existence. On their
demise, he can (only) then select some data made available at their death. (W.T.R. 27-9, 47-8) On this basis
it is difficult to understand how, in the context of
Whitehead's technical theory, justice can be done to
(one can properly interpret) the relation between God
and man which Jesus of Nazareth advocated and exemplified.
More specifically, it seems impossible to do justice
(within the context of Whitehead's theory of actual entities) to the religious insights concerning love, tender
care, companionship and so on. A theory which makes it
impossible to have relations with an entity which has
achieved distinctive individuality, except in the tenuous
sense of using data made available by its demise--suffers
from serious defects.

Consider this situation also from "the side of" a
finite actual entity. In the context of Whitehead's
metaphysical theory no ordinary actual entity can provide data for possible use by God (a) during its process
of self-development or (b) while it exists as a complete
entity. In Whitehead's view there is a very brief process of self-development of an actual entity. When the
process ends the completed entity does not linger. As
such it disappears forthwith. Thus an actual entity
is either coming into being or perishing. It "never

really is" (P.R. 126), in the sense of continuing in a state of distinctive individuality.

The very transcient, hence elusive, nature of an ordinary actual entity renders it an "unlikely" candidate for the status: companion, object of love or tender care, patience--from the point of view of God or any other actual entity.

Some of the difficulties with Whitehead's metaphysical system, noted above, are due to his "brief life" theory of actual entities. (A.I. 223-4) He is well aware of the problem of accounting for endurance. His attempt to deal with the problem of an enduring entity, in his theory of "society", is not adequate. According to this theory, a society is a complex series of brief moments of experience, with a common pattern.[10] One cannot be satisfied with love or companionship directed toward, ultimately, a common pattern!

All these critical comments bring into focus the need to stress, contrary to Whitehead, the experienced fact of enduring, distinctive, individuality which is more complex than what is covered in Whitehead's theory of societies of actual entities.

It is here reported that, actually, and crucially: a human mind is a distinctively individual entity which has numerous moments of experience. In its process of development from infancy, to adolescence, and finally to adulthood (one and the same mind), it undergoes a process of self-development which in due course brings it to a state where it has achieved certain relatively stable characteristics of behavior. Further processes of development may take place but, for all practical purposes, the main features of the mind have been determined. Such a developed mind may continue to exist (endure) for a considerable period--engaging in various activities, some of them relatively new. It is of course the case that sometimes drastic changes occur, for example,because of advanced age. In brief, any person, passing through the years from early infancy to the onset of senility or death, has in a genuine sense, one and the same mind, and experiences vast expansion, and later contraction, of activities and abilities. (See E.R. 60-61, 198, 298, 373-74, 395-96) Given this mind, entity, and its associated body, it is entirely possible to have relations characterized by love, companionship,

ender care, etc. without getting involved in the dif-
iculties (noted above) which are attendant on White-
ead's "brief life" theory of actual entities.

Also, contrary to Whitehead's theory, it is evident
hat there can be a saving of some of what otherwise
ould have been lost--without the necessity of absorp-
ion into God's life--involving the destruction of the
ntity in question.[11] It is possible for a human person
o take initiative in saving what otherwise would have
een lost--in some cases, save an entity in its entirety
-not just some data derived from it. What is of value
n the lives of some men, and in parts of the physical
nvironment, can be preserved as long as life lasts, if
here is proper appreciation of them, and use of avai-
able preservative techniques. Many of the crucial
nsights of Plato have been preserved for a very long
ime, thanks to human appreciation and initiative.

There is an unfortunate implication of "depre-
ation of anything other than God", in the emphasis on
alvation by absorption. Further, is it really a case
f "saving" if what God absorbs is transformed in his
ife? (P.R. 527, 531-32) Whitehead also refers to
eformation (P.R. 527) and transmutation (P.R. 531).
he terms "purged" and "dismissed into triviality" are
lso used. (P.R. 525, 527) In any case, there will be
ome loss of the world's content. According to White-
ead's theory, God saves only what can be saved in
ccordance with his subjective aim. (P.R. 525) Even
ore fundamental is his claim that data are available,
or possible use by God, only after something has been
ost--namely, the complete inner life of a now de-
eased actual entity. (P.R. 336) (See also this volume,
hapter 2.)

Incidentally, it is paradoxical that some devotees
f Whitehead who stress the process aspect of his philo-
ophy, are very anxious to have in God the enduring
resence of all past actual entities in their entirety--
ithout change of any sort. (See this volume, pp. 36-37.)

It will have been noted that a distinction has been
ade between ordinary (finite) actual entities and the
ctual entity God. That such a distinction is funda-
ental becomes increasingly evident as one engages in a
areful examination of Whitehead's philosophy. For
xample, God organizes the entire realm of eternal ob-
ects--no other actual entity does that. In making data

available to others, ordinary actual entities die--go out of existence. On the other hand God, while providing concrete data (i.e., feeling data) does not go out of existence in this process, nor while making eternal objects available for possible use by other actual entities.[12] These differences between God and other actual entities constitute a serious problem for Whitehead in view of his claim that God is not an exception to metaphysical first principles--"He is their chief exemplification." (P.R. 521)

IV

Several <u>conclusions</u> have emerged: We find human beings characterized by (i.e., manifest) love, patience, persuasion, tender care. We have met persons who are termed great companions, fellow sufferers who understand, those who help to save what otherwise would be lost. In a genuine sense they give evidence of having achieved, or at least approximated, the quality "divine". There is good reason to doubt that anyone has ever experienced the extended, enduring, sort of "behavior" which Whitehead is thinking about when he refers to the God actual entity.

In any case, as has just been noted, Whitehead's actual entity God (because of the functions, or lack of them, assigned by Whitehead to actual entities) does not interpret, i.e., cover effectively, some crucial aspects of the divine characteristics manifest by Jesus of Nazareth.

In view of all this, and bearing in mind the awesome, perplexing, technicalities of Whitehead's theory of actual entities,--the difficulties involved in ingression, objectification, subjective form, subjective aim, the category of the ultimate--and so on and on[13]--it seems advisable to consider seriously the possibility of thinking of God primarily in terms of the life and teachings of Jesus, rather than in terms of a theory of actual entities.

It must be emphasized that this suggestion does not involve the abandonment of the essence of Whitehead's approach to God. Whitehead's fundamental reliance is on his religious (moral and metaphysical) insights, i.e., intuitions. The concepts of his technical system are of secondary importance, in the sense

198

hat they are tentative instruments designed to elu-
idate these insights and should be supported, or
ejected, by reference to them.[14] In brief, it is
ere suggested that it is advisable to give priority,
n thinking about God, to concepts such as love, per-
uasion, patience, companionship, fellow sufferer,
xerciser of tender care (in the sense in which they
pply to the life and teachings of Jesus), rather than
o concepts (categories) such as actual entity, ingres-
ion, objectification, subjective aim, subjective form.
s has been noted above, the attempt to set the result
f Whitehead's moral intuitions in the context of his
heory of actual entities does not "work out" except
n a very tenuous fashion. The full meaning of such
ehavior as love, tender care, companionship--is not
dequately covered by the theory of actual entities.
ne further detail remains to be mentioned. Jesus
as engaged in a process of development (as well as
hat of saving some of the things of value in the
orld around about him). Thus a list of appropriate
oncepts, to be used in thinking of God, must include
hat of process of development.

V

The question as to whether there actually is
n "other than human" divine being, with the qualities
hich Whitehead approves, is difficult to settle to
he satisfaction of all who are concerned with it.
ome mystics, some spiritualists, claim to have direct
xperience of such a being. It is well to avoid sweep-
ng dogmatism on either side of the question. One can,
n the last analysis, be content to report, "as of now",
hat he has had such an experience, or he has not.
here is, of course, a qualifying factor: Sometimes,
n the basis of experience of another person's relia-
ility in many instances, one accepts as correct, re-
orts based on the experience of others,--experience
hich is not shared, by the acceptor.

One interesting approach to the problem of a divine
ing was formulated by William James as his theory of
he "divine more".[15] He claimed that it is scientifi-
ally respectable to contend that there is a flow of
nergy coming into our experience through the unconscious.
his energy supports our behavior when it is characterized
y moral excellence. Among such sorts of behavior are,

of course: love, persuasion, tender care, companionship, and so on. Here, then, we find a claim to direct experience of something which is either characterized by the qualities of Jesus of Nazareth, or at least supports them and thus is concerned with them. The exact inner nature of this source of power is not at all clear. This is not revealed in our experience. Hence, it may well be most appropriate to have a theory of God which does not presume to "spell out" in exact detail his nature and function. The "most perceptive experience" of God is usually prepared to recognize the limitations of human understanding when confronted by the vast complexity and obscurity of experience of the reputed divine being.

It may be objected, in opposition to this approach, that one can have justifiable confidence in the considerable amount of detailed exposition obtained by using the categoreal scheme of Process and Reality (pp. 27-42). However, Whitehead is the first to warn against uncritical use of, and reliance on, this categoreal scheme. He has no delusions of grandeur about it, nor fanatical reverence for it. Consider, for example: "Metaphysical categories . . . are tentative formulations of the ultimate generalities" (P.R. 12). "If we consider any scheme of philosophic categories as one complete assertion, and apply to it the logicians' alternatives, true or false, the answer must be that the scheme is false" (P.R. 12).

VI

This chapter is not an abandonment of a rational approach to the problem of God. Rather, in view of the nature of man's experience, it seems wiser to place major emphasis on a few experiential concepts such as love, companionship, tender care (as manifest in the life and teachings of Jesus), rather than speculative metaphysical ones such as actual entity, subjective form, ingression, objectification and so on, which are involved in an attempt to provide a complete system of concepts. Rather it is a case of recognizing the limitations, and relative status, of these categories in dealing with a particular sort of entity, namely the divine being.

Notes

1. R.M. 16-17, 41, 68-70, 75, 154; S.M.W. 266-67, P.R. 521, 525-26; A.I. 213, 215-16.

2. R.M. 16, 41, 72-73, 154-55; S.M.W. 268; P.R. 520, 524-27, 532; A.I. 213, 215-16.

3. R.M. 32-33, 36, 56, 59, 86; S.M.W. 267-69; P.R. 521, 527; A.I. 207, 215, 369, 374; M.T. 140-42, 164, 165.

4. R.M. 51, 56-57; A.I. 214.

5. P.R. 28, 116, 168, 339, 521.

6. R.M. 90, 93-95, 98-100, 104-5, 119, 153-54, 156-58; S.M.W. 243-44, 249-50, 266-69; P.R. 11, 19, 28, 46-48, 50, 54, 70, 73, 75, 104, 134-35, 143, 160-61, 164, 169, 248, 315, 339, 343-44, 352, 373-74, 377, 382, 392, 425, 434, 519-33; A.I. 213-16.

7. Indeed, it would appear that in a genuine sense, Whitehead's metaphysics implies that any actual entity is restricted to the direct experience of its own component elements. (See this volume, pp. 34-35.)

8. R.M. 68-69, 75, 154; S.M.W. 243-44; P.R. 520, 525-26; A.I. 213.

9. P.R. 46-48, 134-35, 521-24, 529-33.

10. P.R. 50-51; A.I. 261; W.T.R. 50-52.

11. P.R. 525, 527, 529-30; W.T.R. 63-66.

12. P.R. 524-25, 527, 532.

13. W.T.R. 18, 24-26, 30-31, 33-35, 69-72, 175-94 This volume: Index.

14. P.R. 6-7.

15. William James, The Varieties of Religious Experience, Longmans, Green, New York, 1929, pp. 507-19.

EPILOGUE

THROUGH 50 YEARS

The chapters that constitute this volume can perhaps only be fully understood, and evaluated, in the context of some information concerning the experiences of the author.

At Christmas 1928 I received a copy of Will Durant's The Story of Philosophy. The exposition and discussion of Plato's philosophy particularly impressed me. As a sophomore at Mount Allison University I decided to "take" some courses in philosophy. The Essentials of Logic by Roy Wood Sellars was my first text.

My first "meeting with" (the writings of) Whitehead occurred in the spring term of 1930 when Religion in the Making was read during a course in the Philosophy of Religion. The professor, Dr. R.B. Liddy, was primarily impressed by Henry Nelson Wieman. I found Whitehead more appealing. That summer, during a couple of rainy days at a resort cottage, Science and the Modern World aroused my interest in the extensive range of Whitehead's insights, and his ability to express himself with vigor and clarity. During the summer of 1932, after a year of graduate study at the University of Toronto, I spent five months in northern Saskatchewan (Canada), and in "spare time" began my continuing attempt to understand Process and Reality. In the fall of 1933 Adventures of Ideas opened new vistas of Whitehead's philosophy. At this time Symbolism, its Meaning and Effect; The Concept of Nature; The Principles of Natural Knowledge appeared on the second hand book table at Brittnels. These volumes became part of my Whitehead collection. I "passed up" The Principle of Relativity because it appeared to be too technical for my competence. Little attention was paid to any of these philosophy of science books at this time.

The academic year 1934-35, at the University of Chicago, was devoted to attempting a Ph.D. thesis on Whitehead's Metaphysics (Ontology and Epistemology) under the supervision of Charles Hartshorne and H.N. Wieman. During 1935-36 I spent part of my time at the University of Toronto revising the thesis. In the second term, I "filled in" as instructor in philosophy and psychology at Waterloo College, Waterloo, Ontario. One Saturday in the late spring of 1936, Gregory Vlastos (then of Queen's University, Kingston, Canada) stopped me in front of Victoria College, Toronto, and asked me why I hadn't gone to Harvard to study with Whitehead. I replied that I had heard rumours of Whitehead's very poor health and extreme unapproachability. Very fortunately for me, Vlastos vigorously debunked both reports. I took his advice and registered at Harvard in the fall of 1936. My "Whitehead as Teacher and Philosopher" (reprinted in Chapter 2 of this volume) is a partial attempt to do justice to some of my experiences during that academic year (see also my "Introductory Essay" in The Wit and Wisdom of Whitehead). In brief, my thesis "Actual Entities: A.N. Whitehead's Theory of Reality" was discussed with Whitehead in weekly individual tutorial sessions.--He then read it and made marginal initialed comments. During that period, I wrote a brief critical note on an article in The Philosophical Review by D. Bidney entitled "Spinoza and Whitehead". Whitehead read it and recommended publication. It appeared in The Philosophical Review, Vol. 47, No. 4 (July 1938) pp. 410-14. This was my first publication dealing with Whitehead's philosophy. (See pp. 106-11 of this volume.)

My appointment as instructor in philosophy and psychology at the University of Western Ontario in 1937 involved a heavy teaching program in all areas of philosophy and introductory psychology. However, by the early 1940s, it was possible to devote summers to the preparation of articles on Whitehead's philosophy. By this time, my interest had extended well beyond the ontology and epistemology of Science and the Modern World, Process and Reality, and Adventures of Ideas. I began more serious investigation of his philosophies of science, civilization (i.e., social, moral and aesthetic issues), history, religion. At this time, I secured copies of The Aims of Education and The Function of Reason. Modes of Thought was also acquired.

In passing, it is perhaps well to explain why, in my articles published during these years in philosophical and psychological journals, much use was made of quotations from Whitehead's writings. The fact of the matter is that his books were not then readily available. Whitehead himself did not have a copy of The Aims of Education for a considerable period in these years. Even after World War II was over, for example, the University of Chicago possessed only <u>one</u> copy of <u>Process and Reality</u>. It was kept under guard in the library and made available for no more than two hours at a time to any one person--on the premises!

At Harvard I had met and had many fruitful discussions with Victor Lowe. The contact with Charles Hartshorne was continued through the medium of correspondence (see Chapter 5 of this volume) and occasional meetings at sessions of the American Philosophical Association. The same has been the case concerning Victor Lowe. After Whitehead died in December 1947, Hartshorne, Lowe and I participated in the memorial session at the Western Division of the American Philosophical Association. This symposium was published as <u>Whitehead and the Modern World</u> (under my editorial supervision).

My <u>Whitehead's Theory of Reality</u> (1952) grew out of the thesis written at Harvard under the supervision of Whitehead. My <u>Whitehead's Philosophy of Civilization</u> (1958) developed journal articles written in and published during my early years at the University of Western Ontario. These books were supplemented by collections of Whitehead's papers and essays for which introductory essays were provided, namely: <u>A.N. Whitehead: The Interpretation of Science</u> (including the series of papers presented to the Aristotelian Society and <u>Whitehead's American Essays in Social Philosophy</u> (including a number of <u>Atlantic</u> essays).

My first book published in the field of Whitehead study, <u>The Wit and Wisdom of Whitehead</u> (1947) occurred when Melvin Arnold, then of the Beacon Press, Boston, saw in <u>Philosophy of Science</u> my collection of Whitehead aphorisms entitled "The Wit and Wisdom of Whitehead". He suggested publication in book form. I expanded the project by suggesting the inclusion of a survey article dealing with Whitehead which had been recently published in the <u>University of Toronto Quarterly</u>. This was done. Subsequently the Beacon Press published <u>Whitehead and the Modern World</u>, <u>Whitehead's Theory of Reality</u> and <u>Whitehead's Philosophy of Civilization</u>.

In 1961 in celebrating the one hundredth anniversary of Whitehead's birth, the Eastern Division of the A.P.A. organized a symposium in which R.M. Palter dealt with Whitehead's Philosophy of Science, W.A. Christian his Metaphysics. I discussed some aspects of his social philosophy. Meanwhile, since the 1920's, interest in most aspects of Whitehead's philosophy developed very rapidly and broadly among philosophers in North America. Yale, Texas, Emory and Claremont, for example, became recognized as centers of Whitehead scholarship. The vast outpouring of articles, and the appearance of many books, occurred. So called "Process Philosophy" and "Process Theology" became prominent features of the North American intellectual environment.

Yet, in the midst of all this--increasingly, it seemed to me--I judged after careful deliberation--that very serious misinterpretations of Whitehead's philosophical ideas were taking place. Worse still, there were serious digressions from the spirit of Whitehead, among some of those who prided themselves on being his disciples.

Chapters in this volume have examined and corrected some of the major errors which have occurred in discussions of Whitehead's philosophy--both technical and non-technical aspects. As to spirit: Whitehead himself was characterized by an exuberant and joyful spirit of adventure in the realms of intellect and value appreciation. He recommended and embodied the creative Hellenic approach to life and deplored excessive emphasis on the restrictions of the Hellenistic pattern of life.

The contrast between Hellenic and Hellenistic, as envisioned by Whitehead (Adventures of Ideas, pp. 132-38, 150), merits careful attention. It is a contrast between Athens and Alexandria. More specifically the Hellenic way of life (and spirit) is characterized by speculation, direct observation of facts, delight.--The Hellenistic approach (or spirit) is that of a scholar who works within rigorous limitations-- addiction to: concentration, thoroughness, investigation of special topics (A.I. 134). In brief, the Hellenic way of life is creative, the Hellenistic is devoted to concentration (A.I. 150).

Whitehead emphasizes the point that both the Hellenic and Hellenistic spirit and way of life are required if there is to be any genuine progress. He is particularly anxious to stress that the Hellenistic approach, if unaccompanied by the Hellenic, "leans towards a fundamental negation" (A.I. 137). It is satisfied with

206

the examination of definite fact, neatly categorized into separate subjects of knowledge. It neglects what is at present beyond the range of clear cut human experience and hence knowledge. Thus while Alexandria conserved,--without the creative Hellenic spirit, this mentality has very serious defects. In all fairness, Whitehead, on the other hand, is prepared to admit that "pure speculation, undisciplined by the scholarship of detailed fact, or the scholarship of exact logic, is on the whole more useless than pure scholarship, unrelieved by speculation" (A.I. 138).

With this by way of background, it is essential to note that among some Whitehead scholars there is a strong tendency to regard his tentative formulation of technical categories (P.R. 27-42) as final, and to adhere rigorously to some preferred, or recommended, pattern of interpretation. They forget that the ultimate foundation of Whitehead's philosophy is, as he points out very definitely, a group of insights (intuitions) concerning the basic factors in the universe as found in comprehensive human experience. Some of these insights have not yet received adequate conceptualization despite continuing efforts to achieve this.

One of Whitehead's remarks concerning "adventure" particularly impressed me: "the most un-Greek thing that we can do is to copy the Greeks. For emphatically they were not copyists" (A.I. 353). I understand Whitehead to mean by "copy": slavishly duplicate, or be excessively or exclusively concerned with, the details of anything the Greeks said or did--without emulating the Greek spirit which generated these particular "things", which are specific reactions to basic situations. As a matter of fact Whitehead, as noted above, had a very favorable attitude toward the creative spirit manifest by the great Greeks--the Hellenic spirit of Plato and the great tragic dramatists for example--the continuing unfettered unrestricted search for fundamentals.

As a matter of fact, Whitehead's own philosophical development was an impressive illustration of the concept: creativity. The journey from Principia Mathematica to Modes of Thought and beyond--is truly a manifestation of the Hellenic spirit. Consider, for instance, the transition from "no metaphysics" of The Concept of Nature to the technical categoreal scheme of Process and Reality pp. 27-42). There is a striking development from the objects and events of his earlier writings in the philosophy of science to his theories of eternal objects and

actual entities. Consider also the difference between
The Principle of Relativity and his philosophy of
civilization, or the chapter in Science and the Modern
World entitled "The Romantic Reaction". It is indeed
significant that Whitehead includes creativity as one
of the three basic ingredients of the "category of the
ultimate". In brief, so-called "process philosophy"
should legitimately be expected to be characterized by
process! Even in late 1947 Whitehead's mind was still
alert and eagerly concerned with new experiences, and
their categorization.

        Increasingly influenced by the Hellenic spirit
of Whitehead (as well as an awareness of the value of
scholarly Hellenistic activities) I embarked on the
adventure of attempting to formulate a philosophic
system which, in general, agrees with many of Whitehead's basic insights, but differs markedly from his
system in some crucial details--because of alternative,
or additional, insights. As a result Experiential
Realism (1973) appeared--and also Modes of Value (1978).

        During the period when I was formulating my
philosophical system (1964--) I was regularly engaged
in discussing Whitehead's philosophy with students and
colleagues at the University of Western Ontario and
elsewhere. Increasingly I became convinced that the
highly technical categories (concepts) of Process and
Reality as outlined in pages 27-42, which apply to
some aspects of human experience with varying degrees
of efficacy--should not be regarded as the final, or
central, point of interest in Whitehead's philosophy.

        This set of categories is paralleled by a set
of relatively non-technical ones which in some respects
do more justice to basic aspects (i.e., basic factors)
found in human experience--than do the technical ones.
In brief, Whitehead "speaks" to specialists in highly
technical concepts and language. He communicates with
all men and women through the medium of relatively
ordinary concepts and language. Full use should be
made of both these channels of communication,--because
Whitehead comes to grips with problems which concern
all people.

        It will have been noted that in these chapters
attempts have been made to clear up misunderstandings
of both Whitehead's (a) technical and (b) non-technical
--concepts and language. However, some strong criticisms

have been offered of Whitehead's treatment of the human person and the nature and function of God, in the context of his technical theory of actual entities. Defects of other sorts, e.g., of expression have also been pointed out.

My *Experiential Realism* and *Modes of Value* illustrate the fact that it is possible to agree with many of Whitehead's basic insights, but to disagree with crucial ingredients of his last philosophical position, because of an appeal to insights which he apparently "missed" and which make an alternate philosophical system at least plausible.

These criticisms and these digressions from the theories of Whitehead should not lead anyone to overlook the fact that Whitehead's spirit and many of his basic insights, and exposition of them, have had a decisive influence on the author of this book. I shall never forget his delight, and his dedication, in the search for new ideas and their implementation--his humility and humaneness in dealing with fellow human beings. When confronted by Whitehead and his philosophy, it was impossible, for any perceptive person, to "crawl off" into some restricted, narrow, corner of intellectual pursuit and thus neglect the vast range of human experience and problems. He focused attention on the complex constitutive inter-relations of all things great and small. He stressed the importance of recognizing the presence of permanence as well as change --the individual as well as the group. The values of civilized living were contrasted with the procedures of barbarism. He concerned himself with both God and the world. Always there was an appeal to one's own immediate experience--made accurate and efficient by careful avoidance of sources of error. For my association with Alfred North Whitehead, I am grateful beyond the power of words to express.

This statement of the background, and course, of over fifty years of reflection on the philosophy of Alfred North Whitehead will perhaps serve to clarify, for some persons, the meaning of the category: Whiteheadian.

NOTE:

I. The following material has been placed in the
    Library of Mount Allison University, Sackville,
    New Brunswick, Canada: A.H. Johnson's

    a) Lecture notes on Whitehead's courses on
       "Cosmologies" (Fall 1936), "Function of
       Reason" (Spring 1937).

    b) Notes on private tutorial sessions with
       Whitehead, Harvard 1936-37.

    c) Ph.D. thesis "Actual Entities: A.N. White-
       head's Theory of Reality" with marginal notes
       by Whitehead, Harvard 1936-37.

    d) Letters from Whitehead, including those re-
       produced in this volume.

    e) Letters from Charles Hartshorne, including
       those reproduced in this volume.

    f) Correspondence with other Whitehead scholars,
       in particular with Victor Lowe and Paul Weiss.

II. To this material will be added:

    g) Statements from Harvard sources, New York Times
       etc. concerning Whitehead's career and demise.

    h) Offprints, reviews etc. concerning Whitehead.

INDEX

(Major occurrences of items)

213